# Shoeing Right

# Shoeing Right

## Advice to Horse Owners
## from a Working Farrier

### DAVID KROLICK

Breakthrough
Publications, Inc.

I dedicate this work
to the horseshoers who strive for excellence
and are willing to share
what they discover.

For information address:
Breakthrough Publications, Inc.
Ossining, New York 10562

Designed by Jacques Chazaud
Illustrations by Kip Carter
Printed in Mexico

ISBN: 0-914327-39-9
Library of Congress Catalog Card Number: 91-075120

99 98 97 96          8 7 6 5 4

# Contents

# Acknowledgements

I gratefully acknowledge the help of these people:

My wife, Geni Krolick, for her editorial help, for encouragement, and for being my friend.

Dr. David G. Wilson, University of Wisconsin, Madison, for allowing me access to the laboratory and for help with the specimen photographs.

Dr. Dean Peterson, Badger Veterinary Clinic, for allowing me the use of radiograph files.

Rhona Johnson, for pulling everything together and turning the words into a book.

Alice Bennett, for a copyedit process that helped bring out my voice in the words.

Kip Carter, for fine artwork.

Dan Block for a day filled with photo opportunities.

My father and mother, Nat and Pauline Krolick, for helping me in innumerable ways, but most importantly by encouraging me to be a freethinking person, self-confident enough to undertake this project.

September Morn, for teaching me how to talk with animals.

The owners who educate themselves and spend their time and money to provide quality care for their horses. It is a fair and honorable pursuit. Your comments about this book are welcomed and can be sent to me: c/o Breakthrough Publications, 310 North Highland Avenue, Ossining, New York 10562.

# 1

---

# General Considerations

Good horse management requires knowledge in many areas. Too often, riding is the only horse-related activity pursued with enthusiasm and commitment. The true equestrian strives for understanding in all aspects of horse care, including nutrition, training, and horse psychology, general stable management, basic veterinary care, and hoof and leg care. The better our understanding of these components, the better equipped we are to make sound horse-care decisions. This is important even for those who hire experts to provide all these services. How else can we wisely choose a stable, a trainer, a veterinarian, and a farrier—or for that matter, the right horse?

This book is not a training manual in farrier science. It's about being an educated consumer. It has been written for people who would like a better understanding of horseshoeing: why it's done, what options are available, what problems and solutions are associated with shoeing, what the owner's role is, and how to identify quality work.

To provide proper care for a horse, a farrier must have and use knowledge and skill in several areas. Above all, a shoer must understand and be skilled at trimming. More than any other process, trimming influences the alignment of the bones of the leg and hoof, as well as determining the amount of stress placed on the tendons and ligaments. The trim directly influences the animal's comfort when worked and can make the difference between a sound horse and a lame one. Nevertheless, this is also an area of weakness for many horseshoers and a skill underrated by many owners.

Correct selection and application of shoes are also important skills. Good shoeing practices can enhance the shock-absorbing qualities of the hoof and avert many problems. Furthermore, to be competent at these primary skills, a farrier must have a working knowledge of the anatomy and physiology of the hoof and leg as well as the dynamics of equine movement.

With few exceptions, horseshoeing schools today offer only a short course (two to fourteen weeks) that teaches the elementary skills needed to accomplish basic shoeing tasks and provides an overview of anatomy and physiology. Without a structured apprenticeship, it is difficult for even the most conscientious person to learn the finer points of the trade. A serious student must actively seek out greater understanding by reading, by attending workshops and seminars, by gaining practical experience, and by finding skilled farriers who are willing to share their expertise. Following this path is time consuming and often expensive, but it is necessary.

Mastering this profession is difficult enough, but putting those skills to work becomes even more complicated because it takes longer to provide quality care. This means that fewer horses can be shod each day, sometimes producing less income. It may also surprise many that shoeing a horse correctly—in the way that least interferes with the natural functioning of the hoof—can increase the likelihood of cast shoes. This creates a dilemma for the shoer, because one measure of a shoer's skill commonly used by owners is how long the shoes stay attached. To maintain a good reputation and avoid callbacks, even a shoer who knows better can be tempted to use a too-small shoe, not fitted full enough at the heels, attached with nails that are placed inappropriately in the hoof in order to keep the shoe on longer. So we see that in addition to skill and expertise, one also needs strength of character and self confidence to excel as a horseshoer.

Consequently, it can be difficult for a horse owner to know whether a farrier is providing competent care. There are no licensing requirements, and long apprenticeships are uncommon. The American Farrier's Association does have a fine voluntary certification program that is a good indicator, but it cannot guarantee professional excellence. Furthermore, some fine craftsmen have not found it necessary to go through the association's certification process. As a result, there is no easy way for a horse owner to identify a skilled, trustworthy, professional horseshoer. Even so, to protect their horses, the burden of determining competence does fall on owners. The choices for owners, then, are to trust blindly, to trust someone else's judgment, or to become educated consumers. Blind trust, of course, has obvious pitfalls. Trusting someone else's judgment (a more experienced horse person, a veterinarian, or a trainer) is successful only if the other person has a sound understanding and is available when needed. You should not assume that a veterinarian (particularly one who is not an equine specialist) has received any training in farrier science. Many schools of veterinary medicine do not cover this subject.

This is not to say that veterinarians, trainers, and experienced horse people are not good sources of information about horseshoeing and hoof care. In fact, they are the best places to begin the search for a farrier, as you seek referrals or references. Furthermore, some veterinarians who specialize in horses have extensive experience and understanding of the principles of horseshoeing. From their ranks come many of the leading experts in hoof and leg problems. But being a professional in one aspect of any field does not by itself make someone qualified in another specialized area of the same field. Owners ultimately have to judge the quality of care their horses are receiving.

Horseshoeing practices can assist or interfere with an owner's attainment of horse-related goals as well as affect the horse's comfort. Quality care can minimize the consequences of poor conformation and avoid problems before they hinder riding. It is clearly in the interest of both horse and rider for the owner to have at least a basic knowledge of the principles of horseshoeing. This knowledge begins with the fundamentals of anatomy and physiology: upon this foundation an understanding of horseshoeing and hoof care can be built. Knowledgeable owners can protect themselves and their horses against incompetence, participate in shoeing-related decisions, and identify problems that arise during the weeks between the shoer's visits.

Furthermore, I hope that understanding the shoeing process will give owners the appreciation and respect for skilled, conscientious shoers that these professionals deserve. For a concerned shoer, nothing can compare with working for an owner who has similar convictions about proper horse care and the knowledge to recognize and implement good practices. We should never forget how totally dependent our horses are on our benevolence and the decisions we make on their behalf. We have been entrusted with a great responsibility. When the horse owner and farrier work together everyone benefits, especially the horses. If this book can contribute to this end, even in small measure, it will certainly have accomplished its purpose.

# 2

---

# Anatomy and Physiology

Understanding the horse's anatomy and physiology is not much different from understanding our own. The basic parts are similar. For instance, ligaments attach bones to bones and tendons connect muscles to bones for a horse or for a person. It is the arrangement that makes the difference. All the parts work together to make it possible for us and our horses to move around. We even derive the energy to function from the same place: nutrients from food combine with oxygen, causing a chemical reaction that gives off energy. The nutrients and oxygen are transported to the muscles through the blood. The muscles use this resulting energy to contract, which moves the skeletal framework. The rest (the soft part) goes along for the ride, whether as part of a 1,000-pound horse or a 150-pound person.

The design differences between horses and humans become apparent when we examine the physical requirements of each species. For instance, the position of the human pelvis and our unusual feet sticking out in front, allow us to stand upright. Our opposable thumbs let us grasp objects with our hands. Unique to horses is their ability to carry their own great weight of a thousand pounds or more across a field at thirty miles an hour. Adding a couple of hundred pounds of saddle and rider hardly slows them down. More impressive still is that such an animal can fling its own mass and its passenger over a five-foot jump, land safely, and ready itself for the next obstacle. Beyond the sheer beauty of the movement, what makes these physical accomplishments so remarkable is that the stresses of concussive impact are withstood time and time again. Thousands of pounds of force are absorbed and dissipated by each hoof and leg as they momentarily bear the entire weight of the animal moving at high speed.

As in any complicated system with many moving parts, there is always the chance of mechanical failure. When any one of the parts functions at less than 100 percent efficiency, extra stress is placed on other parts. A system failure (resulting in lameness) can be attributed to one or more of the following: injury, illness, age, environmental factors, human interference, and genetic predisposition. Some factors on the list can be controlled by us, others cannot. We can lessen the risk of lameness by taking charge of the variables we can control. For instance, horses will eventually get old and rickety, but the deterioration can be slowed through good nutrition and proper exercise. Illness cannot always be avoided, but appropriate inoculations will help. The risk of injury can be greatly reduced by good management and a safe environment. Faulty conformation will limit the functioning of the horse's moving parts, but with correct shoeing we can minimize its impact and help the animal perform up to its best potential.

Understanding horseshoeing is not possible without a basic knowledge of the structures it affects. This requires a closer look at these parts—how they work and how they are arranged.

## MUSCLES

Skeletal muscles, the ones designed to move the body, are connected at one end to a relatively stationary bone. The other end of the muscle is attached to another bone by a long, sturdy cord called a tendon. When the muscle contracts, the tendon pulls the second bone and changes its position relative to the stationary bone. There are always corresponding muscles and tendons on the other side of the bones that can pull them back into their original positions. These opposing muscle forces make it possible to control the extent, speed, force, and smoothness of the movement. A sequence of coordinated muscle contractions and associated bone movements is what lets horses (and humans) walk, trot, and gallop.

We often think of bones as rigid, unalterable rods within the body. In fact, bones are constantly changing and being remodeled. This change is accomplished by two kinds of specialized cells. One, called an osteoblast, secretes a tough protein matrix. Calcium salts then fill the matrix, becoming what we think of as bone material. The introduction of calcium salts to the matrix is called ossification. The other kind of cell, called an osteoclast, secretes a substance that "digests" the protein, releasing the calcium from within. In this way, bone acts as a reservoir of calcium, which is needed for most cell functions. When blood levels of calcium become low, calcium from bones is absorbed and put to use.

There are other reasons for bones to be remodeled. The strain of weight bearing will stimulate more protein matrix to be laid down and then filled with calcium. Therefore the thickness and strength of a bone is affected by the amount of work it has to do. If weight bearing is uneven, as in a horse with poor conformation, one side of the bone will become substantially thicker than the other. The whole process is gradual, but it is important because it keeps bones only as heavy as necessary while offering strength where the strain is.

There is also a mechanism for the bones of foals to grow longer. This growth happens at a thin area of cartilage between the main shaft of a bone and the bulbous ends called the epiphyses (fig. 2.1). These growth spots are called epiphyseal plates or, more commonly, growth plates. At these plates cartilage cells multiply, pushing the epiphyses farther away and making the shaft longer. The cartilage is then replaced with

## BONES

**Figure 2.1** The wavy line near each bone's end, called the epiphyseal plate or growth plate, is the place where the bones of young animals grow in length. Eventually each epiphyseal plate ossifies (closes), and the end (epiphysis) and the shaft become one.

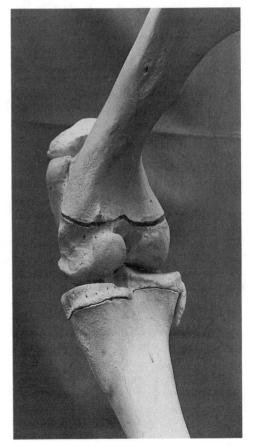

bone matrix by osteoblasts. When calcium salts fill the matrix, bone is created.

How fast and how straight a bone develops is affected by many variables. Heredity plays the leading role, but nutrition and weight distribution are major factors. Nutritionally deficient foals will have less bone growth and become smaller horses (as well as having other problems). Good, balanced feed management encourages optimum growth and will avoid nutritionally caused pathological conditions affecting the bones.

Weight distribution influences bone development because it has a direct effect on the growth plates. Even, balanced pressure around the growth plate will result in symmetrical bone development. Uneven weight bearing, caused by hereditary growth patterns or hoof imbalance, will cause asymmetrical pressure at the growth plate. As a result, the new cartilage cell growth, which will later be replaced by bone, cannot be evenly distributed (fig. 2.2). When one side of a bone shaft grows slightly longer than the other, the angle of the bone's end (epiphysis) is altered. This means that the surface of the bone no longer meets the surface of the adjoining bone in the way it was designed to do. No matter what the reason, if a joint grows to maturity this way, there is a permanent conformation flaw.

The solution is, when possible, to avoid or at least eliminate the cause before the bone matures. Although few horses are totally straight and symmetrical, proper nutrition, hoof care, and basic veterinary care will go a long way toward achieving this ideal. When these fail, more drastic and expensive approaches are possible, though without guaranteed results. One method is

**Figure 2.2** Two views of the joint between the cannon bone and the long pastern bone: An evenly developing joint (left); note that the two bones form a straight line. As a result of uneven weight distribution (right), the epiphysis develops unevenly. The two bones do not form a straight line, and the cannon bone tilts to the right.

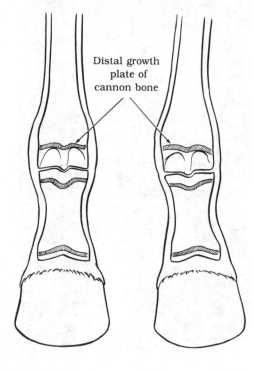

Distal growth plate of cannon bone

called epiphyseal stapling. In this procedure, a steel staple is inserted into the bone across the growth plate at the point where growth is the greatest (fig. 2.3), which stops growth there and allows the other side to catch up, resulting in a more symmetrical bone. The staple is then removed.

Epiphyseal stapling cannot affect conformation once the growth plates have closed. Growth plates themselves naturally undergo ossification, which ends the possibility of growth. Once the epiphyseal plates close, attempting to modify conformation can cause a variety of problems with little or no chance of positive results. For this reason, it is important to know when ossification is complete. Figure 2.4 shows the timing of ossification for the bones of the lower leg.

Another way the shape of a bone changes is by exostosis, which occurs when the bone's protective skin, the periosteum, is bruised, torn, irritated, or damaged in any way. As a repair measure, calcium is deposited at the site of the injury. Calcification of this sort results in a hard lump that can often be felt through the skin (fig. 2.5). Depending on the location of the lump, lameness can occur. When the lump does not interfere with movement or cause internal irritation, however, it is nothing more than a cosmetic flaw or blemish.

Bones perform other functions beyond their job of supporting the body. For example, their core, called bone marrow, plays an important role in the formation of red and white blood cells, hemoglobin, and the platelets needed to make blood clot. Details of how the body systems work together to make such a fascinating creature as a

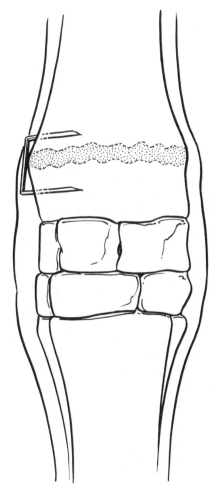

**Figure 2.3** In epiphyseal stapling, a steel staple is surgically placed across the epiphyseal plate at the point of greatest growth. This allows the growth around the rest of the bone to catch up. Courtesy of Dr. David G. Wilson.

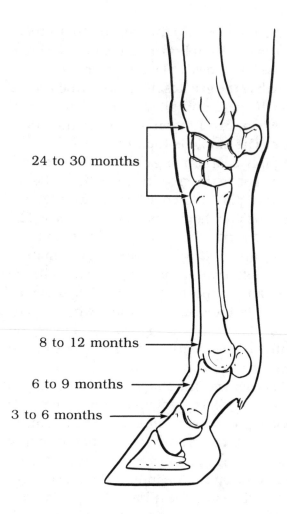

24 to 30 months

8 to 12 months

6 to 9 months

3 to 6 months

**Figure 2.4** The approximate ages growth plates close. These ages will vary somewhat with different breeds.

horse are worth knowing, but are of course beyond the scope of this book. I encourage additional reading.

When we consider hoof care, specific bones are directly involved. Starting at the hoof and going up, they are the coffin bone, navicular bone, short pastern bone, long pastern bone, proximal sesamoid bones (two), cannon bone, and splint bones (two) (figs. 2.6 and 2.7). The positions of these nine bones are the same on the front and hind legs. Continuing up the limbs, the arrangement begins to vary between front and hind legs (fig. 2.8). The knee of the front limb includes seven or occasionally eight small bones. The hock comprises six bones. One must know the names and relative positions of the major bones in order to converse and participate with a veterinarian or farrier in dealing with lameness, disease, and hoof-care alternatives.

Except for the attachment between splint bones and cannon bone, a fibrous capsule surrounds each meeting place of two or more bones. The capsule and its associated structures connect the bones to each other and reduce friction so as to protect the bone ends. In addition, if the energy of muscles is to act on the skeleton and produce movement, a strong connection between muscles and bones is needed. The material that composes all these connecting structures is classified as connective tissue. Though it takes several different forms, it is always tough and resilient. Many parts of the body are at least partially made of connective tissue, including bones (the matrix that the calcium salts fill). The other connective tissue structures that are important for understanding horses and horseshoeing are tendons and ligaments.

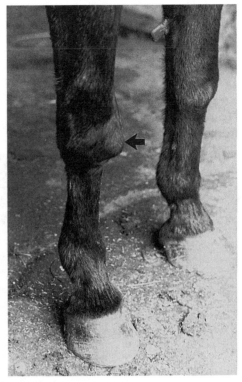

**Figure 2.5** This horse fell to its knees on a hard surface. The bone's covering was damaged, and a permanent calcified lump formed (arrow) as an internal repair measure. Exostoses can occur on any damaged bony surface.

## JOINTS

Where two hard bones meet, there is the potential for great friction and wear. The meeting places, called joints, are specially designed to combat these destructive forces. The bone ends meeting at the joint are covered with smooth cartilage, and the entire area is also surrounded by a layer of fibrous cartilage and ligaments. This tough, durable covering creates a sealed capsule to protect the bones of the joint and hold them in their proper positions. The inner layer is a thin membrane that has the important job

**Figure 2.6** The bones of the lower front leg: (a) from the front; (b) from behind.

**(a)**

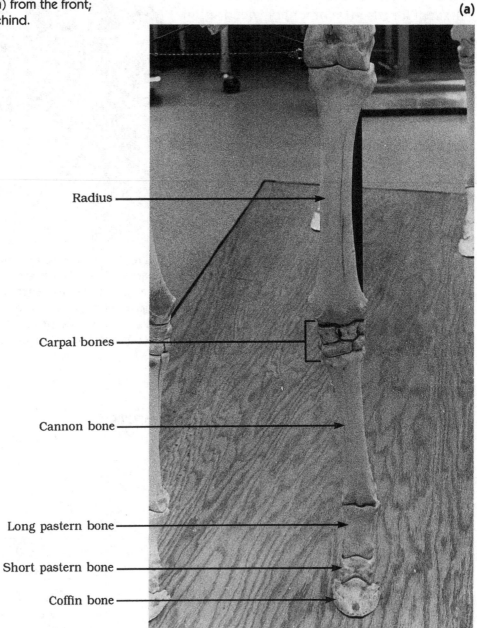

Radius

Carpal bones

Cannon bone

Long pastern bone

Short pastern bone

Coffin bone

(b)

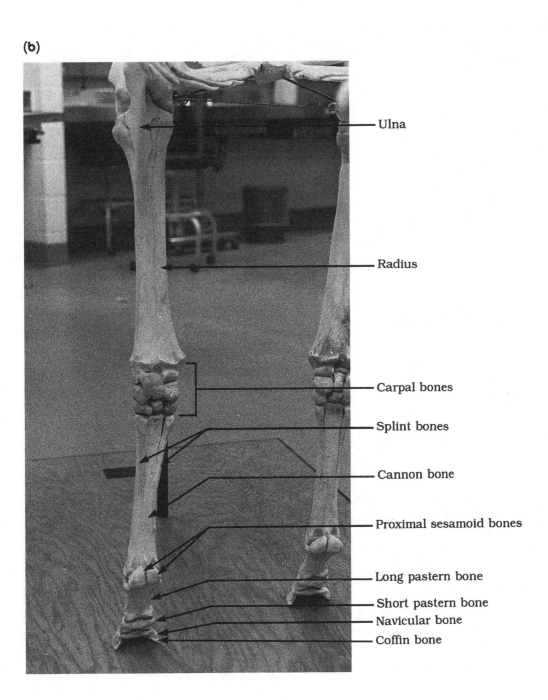

- Ulna

- Radius

- Carpal bones

- Splint bones

- Cannon bone

- Proximal sesamoid bones

- Long pastern bone

- Short pastern bone
- Navicular bone
- Coffin bone

**Figure 2.7** The bones of the lower hind leg: (a) from behind; (b) from the side.

**(a)**

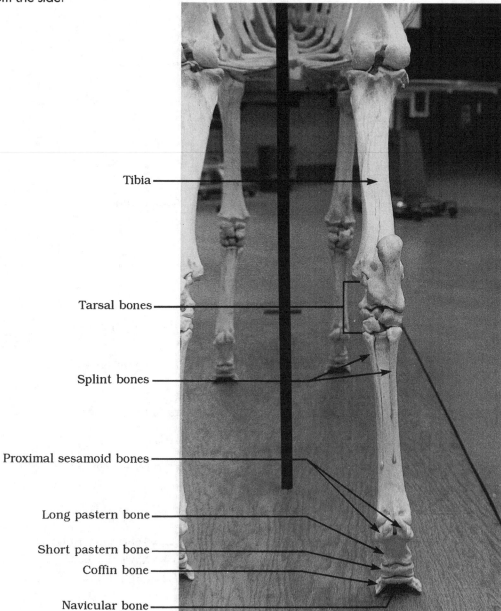

Tibia

Tarsal bones

Splint bones

Proximal sesamoid bones

Long pastern bone

Short pastern bone

Coffin bone

Navicular bone

(b)

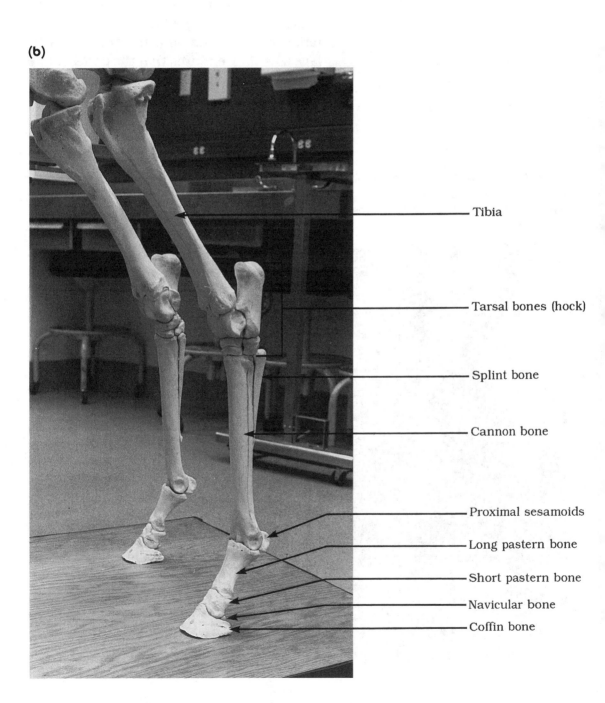

Tibia

Tarsal bones (hock)

Splint bone

Cannon bone

Proximal sesamoids

Long pastern bone

Short pastern bone

Navicular bone

Coffin bone

of secreting a lubricant called synovial fluid. Like other liquids, synovial fluid cannot be compressed. Because the joint capsule is sealed, a layer of fluid remains between the bones even under the pressure of weight bearing. The synovial fluid acts as a cushion, and combined with the smooth cartilage covering, ensures that the bones make virtually no contact with each other. Not only does this cushion eliminate most wear, but each cushion at each joint absorbs some of the concussion caused by hooves hitting the ground. Joints are by far the best self-lubricating, hydraulic shock-absorbing system ever made (except perhaps a horse's hoof).

**Figure 2.8** (a) The bones of the front leg from the shoulder blade down; (b) the bones of the hind leg from the hip down.

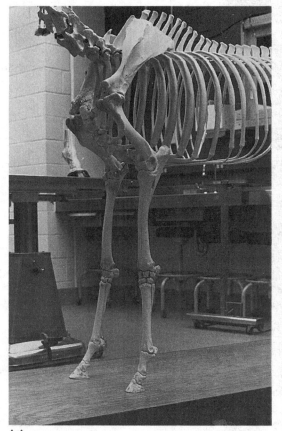

(a)

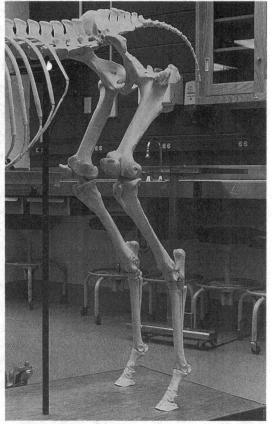

(b)

Another place where friction must be controlled is the bony surfaces that tendons pass over. Tendons are strong, inelastic cords pulled back and forth by contracting muscles. Without a friction-reducing mechanism, they would fray and eventually tear. Small, soft fibrous sacks called bursas are found at the wear points between the tendons and hard, protruding bony surfaces. Additionally, portions of each long tendon are wrapped in a protective covering called a synovial sheath. Like the joint capsule lining, both the bursas and the sheaths secrete synovial fluid to lubricate the area, substantially reducing friction.

Tendons attach muscles to bones. When a muscle contracts, the inflexible tendon pulls a bone. To do this, tendons have to be strong enough to withstand all the power of a big, bulky horse muscle. The muscles that give strength to the legs are all up near the body. In fact, there are no muscles below the knee in the front legs or below the hock in the hind legs, but there are tendons (fig. 2.9) which act as extensions of the muscles by attaching them to the bones in the lower leg. As the muscles contract they pull the bones, which thereby take advantage of the strength of the big muscles without being impeded by their size.

Consider the shape of a horse's leg—thick and muscular near the body but slender toward the hoof. Even though the lower leg is thin, it is extremely powerful. The whole arrangement is very auspicious. A horse would not be a graceful runner if the size of that meaty shoulder and thigh extended down to the hoof. Each leg would weigh hundreds of pounds and be subject to substantial wind resistance. Slender,

## TENDONS

aerodynamic design is made possible by tendons.

There are two basic categories of tendons: flexor tendons and extensor tendons. Movement takes place at a joint where two (or more) bones meet. As the name implies, the action of a flexor tendon is such that, when pulled by its muscle, the bone it is attached to will pivot at its joint and draw up in a flexing motion. In flexion, the angle between the bones gets smaller. An extensor tendon has the opposite effect: the angle between the bones becomes larger. When pulled, the bones are extended into a straighter position. In some cases the joint hyperextends, which is called dorsal flexion. An example of dorsal flexion occurs in the fetlock joint, which extends beyond a straight 180-degree angle.

The major tendons are shown in figure 2.10. Because tendons can do only one thing—transfer the pull of muscles—it is

**Figure 2.9** A postmortem cross section of the lower leg. Note that there are no muscles, only bones and connective structures.

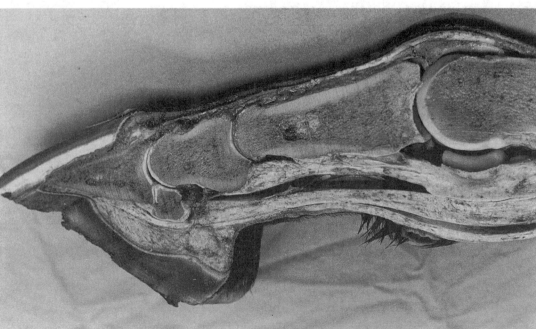

LEFT FORE LEG

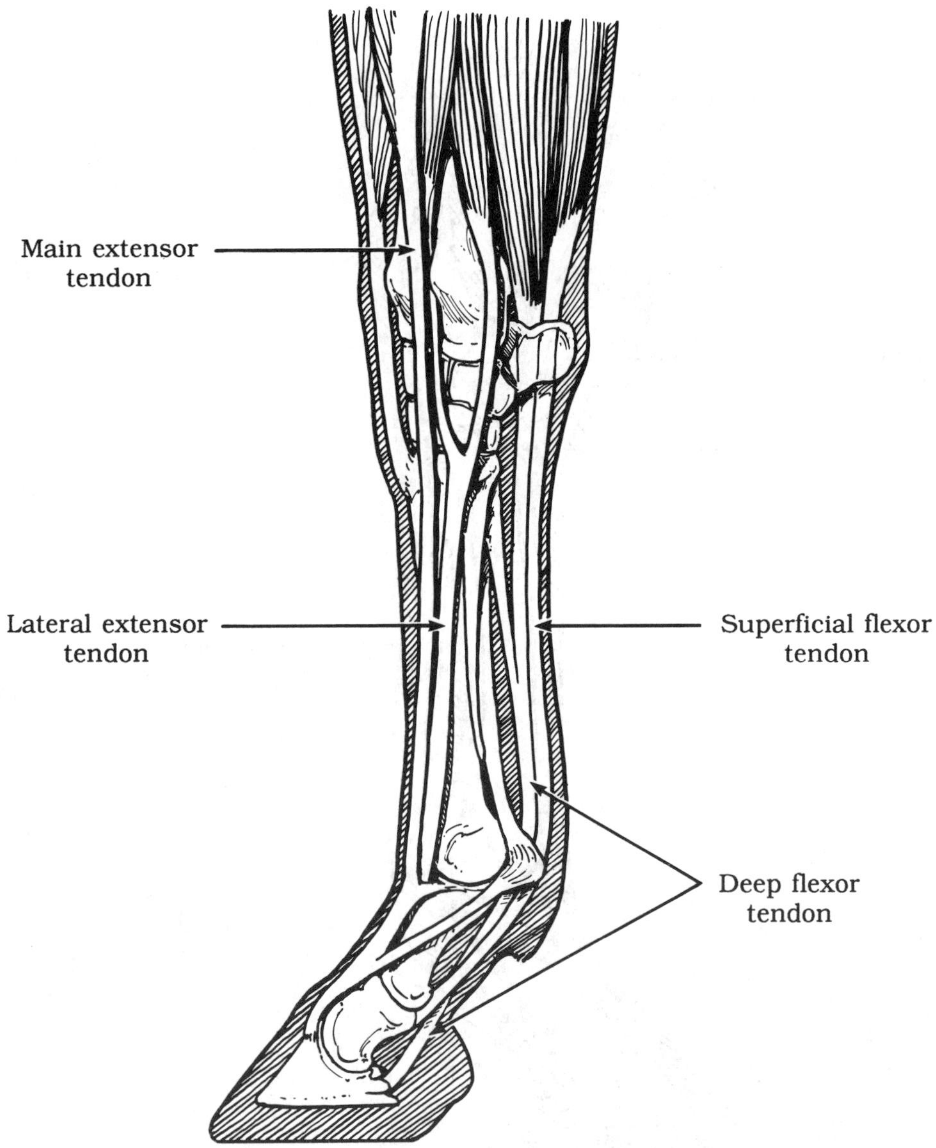

Main extensor
tendon

Lateral extensor
tendon

Superficial flexor
tendon

Deep flexor
tendon

**Figure 2.10** The major tendons of the lower front leg (above) and hind leg (next page), spread out for identification.

LEFT HIND LEG

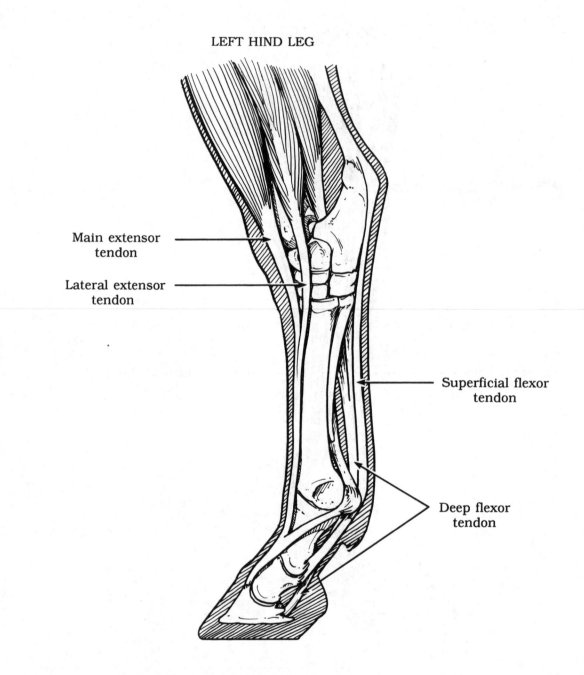

Main extensor
tendon

Lateral extensor
tendon

Superficial flexor
tendon

Deep flexor
tendon

**Figure 2.10** The major tendons of the lower
front leg (previous page) and hind leg (above),
spread out for identification.

generally easy to figure out what effect each one has. Tendons on one side pull bones one way, and tendons on the other side pull them back.

Ligaments, though similar to tendons, are support structures rather than direct aids to movement. They join bones to bones. Unlike tendons, which have straight fibers, the fibers that compose ligaments are kinked, giving them a slightly elastic quality. This is important because ligaments must be somewhat flexible and allow joints to move. In addition, each joint must also be restricted to the specific movement it was designed to perform. To accomplish this, the numerous ligaments at each joint take the form of cords, bands, and fibrous sheets.

Many ligaments working together make it possible for a horse to stand with almost no muscular effort, so horses can sleep standing up. This group of ligaments is called the stay apparatus. The suspensory ligament, the largest ligament in the leg, plays a major role in this arrangement. It is a strong, thick oval cord, and its position behind the fetlock keeps this joint from sinking to the ground (fig. 2.11).

Furthermore, because of their slightly elastic nature, ligaments, particularly the suspensory ligament, will stretch during weight bearing, allowing the fetlock to hyperextend. This way much of the energy of impact is not lost but can be reused. As the weight load is lifted, the elastic structures spring back to their normal positions, helping to propel the leg along in its stride. The horse is not only beautiful and strong, but energy-efficient as well. The complex interrelated structures are a masterpiece of

## LIGAMENTS

engineering, as they must be for the horse to do what through history has been essential for its survival: to run.

## THE HOOF

The primary job of the hoof is to act as the intermediary between the ground and the horse's skeletal framework. The force of gravity exerted on the great mass of the animal travels down the bony column of the leg to the coffin bone. Inside the hoof, the coffin bone is attached to the front two-thirds of the hoof wall. The burden of weight bearing is applied to the hoof wall, which is the primary contact with the ground. The hoof withstands this enormous pressure because of its conical shape and the vertical horn tubules that compose its wall.

The back third of the hoof wall also attaches to a surface. It does not, however, bind directly to the coffin bone like the front two-thirds. Instead, the hoof wall is securely fastened on either side to flexible structures made of cartilage, called the lateral cartilages. The side of each wing-shaped lateral cartilage is attached to the inside of the hoof wall, and the bottom of the cartilage to the side of the coffin bone (fig. 2.12). The top of the cartilage wing rises above the coronary band on both sides of a hoof and is flexible enough to be compressed by finger pressure. This arrangement allows the back portion of the hoof to expand and contract under weight bearing. The expansion and contraction constitute a portion of the hoof's ingenious shock-absorbing system.

In addition to the hoof wall, the frog also bears some of the horse's weight. The frog and the fibrous plantar cushion above it absorb some of the shock as they are

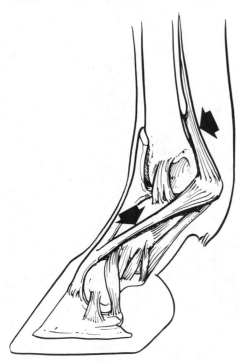

**Figure 2.11** The suspensory ligament (arrows) supports the leg, keeping the fetlock from sinking to the ground. Acting together, the major ligaments allow a horse to stand with almost no effort.

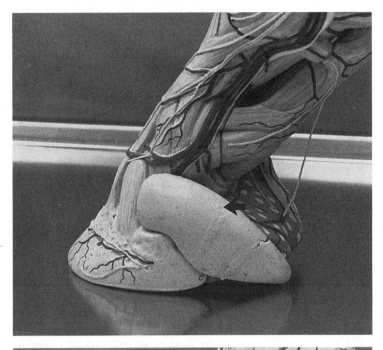

**Figure 2.12** (top) This model demonstrates the position of the lateral cartilage (arrow); (bottom) The top of the lateral cartilages (arrow) extends above the level of the hoof and can be felt through the skin on both sides of each foot.

squashed between the ground and the coffin bone. The hoof wall is pushed outward as weight transfers directly from the descending bony column of the leg. The important attachment of the coffin bone to the inside of the hoof must be flexible, yet strong enough to hold up under these extreme conditions. The attachment structures, called laminae, manage this feat because of their exceptional design. The entire weight of the animal is suspended by an overlapping dovetail of vascular tissue. Looking like the gills of a mushroom, the many folds of the laminae have been estimated to create several square feet of contact between bone and hoof wall (figs. 2.13 and 3.2).

As the horse's weight bears down on the hoof, the spaces within the hoof are compressed. Blood accumulated in the small vessels is squeezed out and pushed, against some resistance, into veins heading back toward the heart. This has two valuable results. First, it solves the problem of how

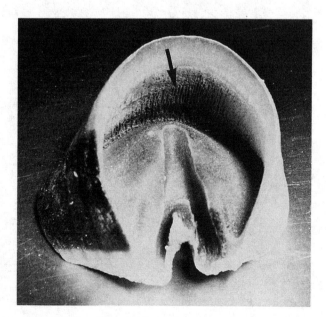

**Figure 2.13** Inside view of the hoof wall, showing the laminae (arrow).

to get the blood moving against gravity when it is too far from the chest to be pushed by the pumping of the heart. Returning to the heart and lungs, the blood picks up more oxygen to be recirculated around the body. And second, the action has a substantial hydraulic shock-absorbing quality.

The only bone besides the coffin bone that is completely housed within the hoof is the navicular bone. Additionally, the bottom portion of the short pastern bone is within the hoof, where it articulates with the top of the coffin bone. These three bones meet, with the navicular behind and slightly below the joint of the coffin and short pastern bones (fig. 2.14).

The navicular bone is notable for the amount of trouble it has caused horses and horse owners. This relatively small bone has a lubricating bursa to protect the deep flexor tendon that passes under it before attaching to the bottom of the coffin bone

**Figure 2.14** Postmortem cross section of a hoof.

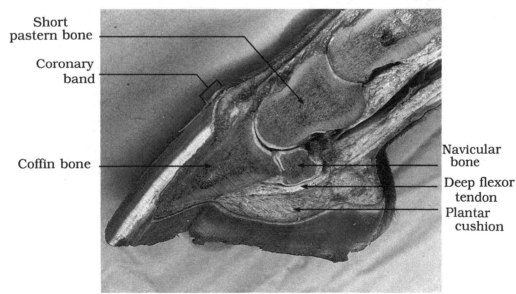

Short pastern bone

Coronary band

Coffin bone

Navicular bone

Deep flexor tendon

Plantar cushion

(fig. 2.14). Its position makes it a fulcrum against which the deep flexor tendon exerts substantial pressure. Everything in the hoof is, of course, under a great deal of stress, and the navicular bone and bursa are no exception. When a problem arises in the navicular bone, the bursa, or the portion of the flexor tendon in this area, it is called navicular disease. This condition is discussed further in chapter 7.

All parts of the hoof below the coronary band that can be seen from the outside are dead tissue with no circulating blood, referred to as insensitive structures (fig. 2.15). This is why the horn material of the hoof wall can be cut, filed, and nailed without doing harm. Likewise, the exposed sole and frog can be carefully pared with a knife without causing pain or blood flow.

For every insensitive structure, however, there is a corresponding living structure inside the hoof. The sensitive sole and sensitive frog generate and are immediately

**Figure 2.15** The bottom of a hoof with insensitive structures identified.

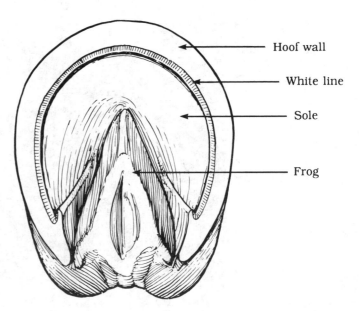

Hoof wall

White line

Sole

Frog

above their insensitive counterparts. There are sensitive and insensitive laminae, and the coronary band is the living structure that generates the insensitive horn material of the hoof wall.

In addition to its shock-absorbing, support, and circulatory functions, the hoof provides traction on many surfaces. The hoof wall generally protrudes beyond the sole to dig into soft ground. Although the sole itself is mostly for protection of internal parts, the frog has special fat glands that help keep it flexible, not only for shock absorbing, but for good traction on hard surfaces as well.

When everything is working correctly, the hoof is a major contributor to a horse's health and athletic ability. It is easy to see the logic in the maxim "No foot, no horse."

## CONFORMATION

Much has been said (and will be said) about correct conformation. What does it mean to be conformationally correct? What does it look like, and why is it so important?

Webster's Unabridged Dictionary defines conformation as "the structure or form of a thing as determined by the arrangement of its parts." Although the concept of conformation is important regarding the entire animal, it is the conformation of the legs and hooves that relates most directly to horseshoeing and will be discussed in this section. The design of the legs as it affects soundness and athletic ability should be a priority for any serious horse person. A pretty animal, or one that is just the right size and shape for a specific job but can do no work because of lameness is obviously of little use and can bring only disappointment.

There is a long continuum between conformation that is close to the ideal and conformation that is so poor as to definitely cause lameness. Moving along this continuum, the first quality lost is efficiency of movement, and the second is the ability to hold up under stress. Exactly how inefficient the movement is or at what level of stress a mechanical breakdown will occur depends on how far from ideal the structure is.

Let us consider the flight path of the leg. A leg that travels through its arc on only one plane—straight ahead—uses much less energy than one that swings to the inside or outside during its stride. The leg's straight path means it travels the shortest possible distance. When we consider a single stride, the difference in energy expended may seem negligible, but multiplied by thousands upon thousands of similar movements, it becomes substantial. The greater the deviation in flight pattern, the more energy is wasted. If two horses with equal ability and conditioning are doing the same work, the one with the least efficient movement will tire first.

However, using more energy can lose its importance if the horse's level of activity never approaches the limit of its physical ability. Thus a horse that could never compete in an endurance race because of conformation flaws may be perfectly serviceable for leisurely trail rides.

Nevertheless, when the flight pattern of a hoof deviates significantly from the norm, other problems may arise. For instance, in overreaching, one or more hooves will touch or strike other limbs during movement. This type of interference problem can cause cuts, bruises, and even bone damage, resulting in exostosis at the site. The horse may also be prone to stumbling and casting its shoes.

Another serious concern regarding faulty conformation is the amount of extra, unbalanced stress placed on joints, tendons, ligaments, and the internal parts of the hoof. Every horse has limits that when surpassed will strain or damage these critical structures. The outward manifestation is lameness. Good conformation or light use may mean that these limits are never reached. In the long run, the amount of work a horse can do while remaining sound is greatly a product of its conformation.

Many of the problems associated with conformation flaws can be improved if a horse wears specialized shoes to shift weight bearing or change the flight pattern of the legs (see chap. 8). In a mature horse, however, these corrective shoes will not bring a self-sustaining resolution of a conformationally caused problem. The problem returns when the shoes are removed. If improvement in a mature animal becomes permanent, the problem was not conformational to begin with. In these cases the real cause has been removed, by either improved management, better riding practices, training, properly fitted tack, or attaining more suitable balance through trimming. Trimming is discussed in chapter 5.

Some aspects of conformation vary from breed to breed and horse to horse. Thick, heavy-boned legs, and hooves the size of dinner plates would certainly be considered a flaw on a thoroughbred intended for racing, but they are a necessity on a two-thousand-pound draft horse (fig. 2.16). The point is that in many ways conformation is relative. Length of legs, neck, and back, as

**Figure 2.16** Conformation is relative to the animal and its use. Heavy-boned legs and large feet are only an advantage in a draft horse.

well as flexibility of the joints, overall size, and bulkiness of muscles, are all factors that can be appraised only in relation to the job the animal will perform. There are, however, some basic rules that hold true in nearly every situation. In all cases the significance of a flaw will have to be measured against the work required.

## Front Legs

In a horse with ideal conformation, a plumb line dropped from the point of the shoulder will define a straight line down the center of the leg and hoof (fig. 2.17). Deviation from this can take several forms. Legs that are straight down to the pastern but have feet that point in or out—called toeing in or toeing out—are a flaw frequently seen (fig. 2.18). Another common flaw is a stance in which the hooves are closer together or farther apart than the shoulders (fig. 2.19). A base-narrow or base-wide stance and toeing in or out cause inefficient gaits and add stress to joints.

Generally, during movement a base-narrow stance or toed-in conformation will cause the hoof to swing toward the outside, away from the midline of the animal. The reverse is true for base-wide or toed-out horses; the hoof swings in, toward the midline and the leg on the other side. When severe, base-wide and toed-out conformation can cause interference problems.

Problems at the level of the knee can be even more serious. A single plumb line should bisect the bones both above and below the knee. If instead the line representing the bones above the knee is parallel to the line below the knee, the horse has offset knees (fig. 2.20). The bones above and below the knee can also be out of alignment in other ways, some of which also occur in people. For instance, horses can be knock-kneed or bowlegged (fig. 2.21).

Similar to being offset, as viewed from the side, the bones above the knee can be forward of (over at the knee) or behind (calf-kneed) the bones below the knee (fig. 2.22). All the knee conformation problems described are very limiting, and horses with these problems do not generally hold up well under stress.

From behind, a plumb line should drop straight down the center of the leg and hoof (fig. 2.23). Hind-leg flaws also include base-wide and base-narrow stances. Other common flaws are being cow-hocked or bowlegged (fig. 2.24). Being cow-hocked, in which the hocks are close but the fetlocks are not, should not be confused with having close but parallel cannon bones. Close but parallel cannon bones can be an acceptable conformation, especially in heavier horse breeds.

From a side view, generally the cannon

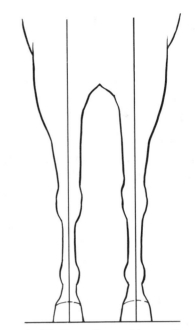

**Figure 2.17** Front legs with good conformation. Note that the plumb line evenly bisects the leg and hoof.

## Hind Legs

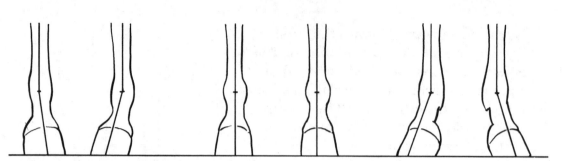

**Figure 2.18** Toed-in conformation (left),
correct conformation (center),
and toed-out conformation (right).

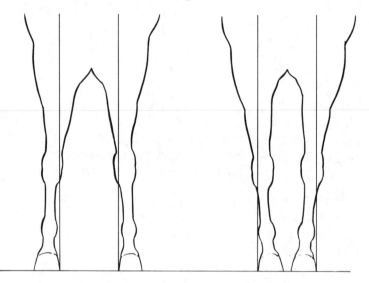

**Figure 2.19** Base-wide stance (left)
and base-narrow stance (right).

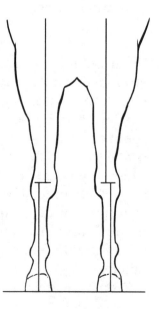

**Figure 2.20** Offset knees.

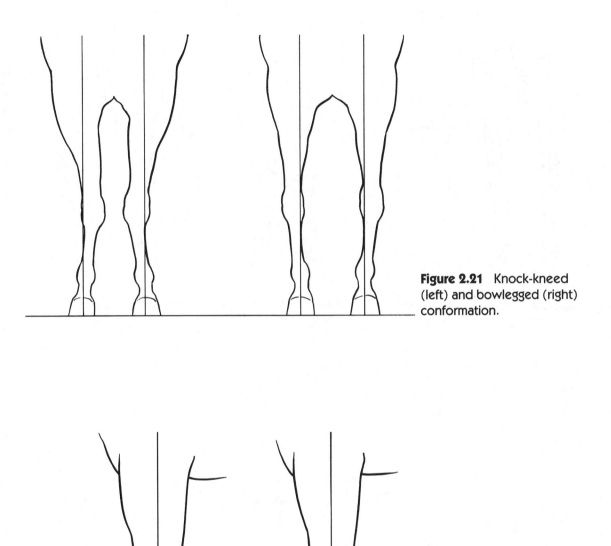

**Figure 2.21** Knock-kneed (left) and bowlegged (right) conformation.

**Figure 2.22** Calf-kneed (left) and over at the knee (right) conformation.

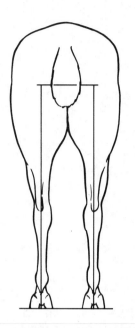
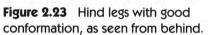

**Figure 2.23**  Hind legs with good conformation, as seen from behind.

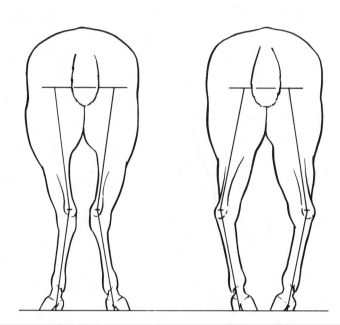

**Figure 2.24**  Cow-hocked (left) and bowlegged (right) conformation.

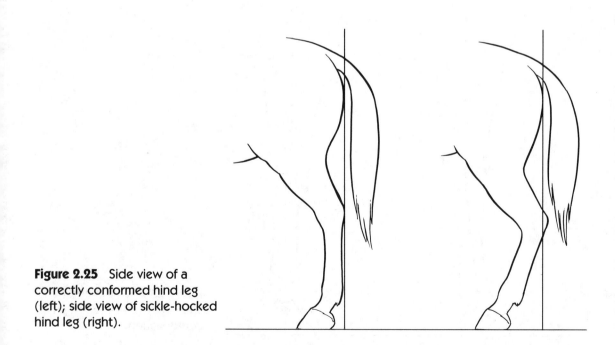

**Figure 2.25**  Side view of a correctly conformed hind leg (left); side view of sickle-hocked hind leg (right).

Front hoof

Hind hoof

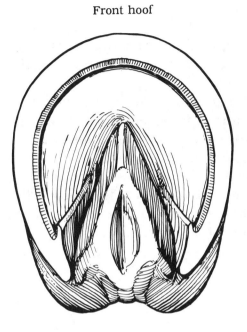
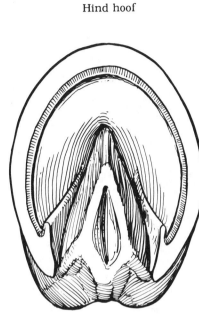

**Figure 2.26** Comparison of an average front hoof (left) and an average hind hoof (right). The hind hoof is generally more oval than round and has a more concave sole.

bone is considered correct when it is perpendicular to the ground. However, many western performance horse trainers prefer animals with hind cannon bones that point slightly forward, a condition referred to as being sickle-hocked (fig. 2.25).

The ideal hoof is nearly symmetrical—not square, too narrow, or excessively pointed. The front hooves are larger and rounder and have flatter soles than the hind hooves (fig. 2.26). Both the overall size of the hoof and the thickness of the hoof wall should be in proportion to the size of the animal. Consequently, no measurement of size or thickness is correct for all horses. The true test is how well the horse's feet hold up to the task of supporting its weight.

In general, a horse's legs and feet are supposed to distribute weight evenly through

## The Ideal Hoof

each joint, down the bony column, and around the surface of each hoof. This allows a straight flight pattern, and the hooves will land squarely, not bearing weight first on one side of the hoof and then on the other.

It is the goal of horseshoeing to match nature's intent as closely as possible. This usually means nothing more than balanced trimming and proper shoeing. When this is not sufficient, special shoes are used to help relieve the stress by distributing the weight more evenly and altering the flight pattern to achieve comfort and safety.

# 3

---

# When to Trim
# and Shoe

Just as human fingernails and toenails are constantly growing out from the cuticle, hoof wall is constantly growing down from the coronary band (fig. 2.14). If the animal is conformationally correct and moves squarely, its hooves will wear evenly and naturally maintain good balance. In fact, if the amount of wear on an unshod horse's hooves is equal to the amount of growth, it may appear that no growth is taking place. This horse will require very little attention from the farrier.

Most horses, however, are not conformationally perfect and are worked more at one time than another, over varying surfaces. The amount of use and the type of ground significantly affect hoof care requirements. More use and hard or rocky ground will wear the hooves faster, and shoes will probably be needed. Conversely, less use and soft footing will allow the feet to become too long, and they will need to be trimmed more often.

It is more common for horses' hooves to grow either faster or more slowly than the rate at which the hoof walls wear. Furthermore, animals with even mild conformation flaws will wear their hooves down unevenly. If we examine our own boot heels, many of us will find uneven wear. So it is with a horse, and when one side of the hoof wears down, the unevenness can become more and more pronounced. When this happens, the imbalance will stress some of the internal structures and ultimately can cause lameness.

When hoof growth cannot keep up with wear, the hooves may become so short that the horse is bearing most of its weight on its soles, which are then prone to bruising. Because of the discomfort, this horse seems to be "walking on eggs." Another horse may grow excessive toe length while its relatively thinner heels break down (fig. 3.1). When this happens its hoof angle becomes so low that strained tendons may become a problem. Proper hoof angle is discussed in chapter 5.

## HOOF GROWTH PATTERNS

The hoof wall is not the solid molded mass it appears to be. The bulk of the wall is made up of many tiny vertical tubes called horn tubules (fig. 3.2). This miracle of na-

**Figure 3.1** Excessive toe length and low heels cause difficult breakover and place extra stress on tendons.

**Figure 3.2** An enlarged cross section showing the structure of the hoof wall horn material and the laminar attachment.

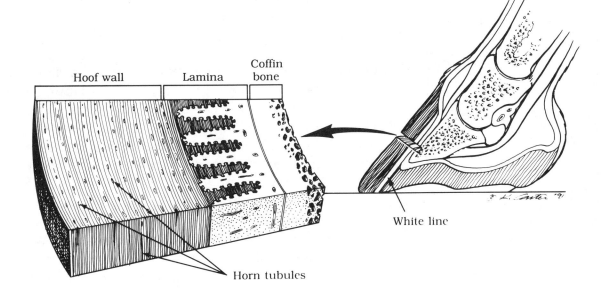

Hoof wall   Lamina   Coffin bone

White line

Horn tubules

ture allows different portions of the hoof to grow at different rates. The controlling factor of this varied growth is circulation of the blood. As pressure is applied to a part of the hoof wall, the circulation in the coronary band directly above is stimulated. The increased blood supply and the nutrients it carries encourage growth. In the wild this allows a horse whose hooves wear unevenly to compensate somewhat with extra growth where needed. It is an excellent system, although human intervention has compromised the benefits, particularly for a shod horse.

Isolated areas of faster growth are more pronounced on a shod horse because hoof wear is prevented. An animal in fairly good balance at the time of shoeing may be out of balance a few weeks later. As lateral (side-to-side) and front-to-back balance changes, so does the quality of movement as well as the animal's comfort and self-confidence. A horse that is kept consistently balanced and lands squarely will have fairly even hoof growth. The key word is "consistently." It takes persistent care to establish even growth and maintain balance.

## SHOEING INTERVALS

The rate of hoof growth depends on many factors. Heredity, nutrition, amount of exercise, wet or dry conditions, general health, and age all constitute pieces of the puzzle. Thus, two horses sharing a pasture and receiving identical care can have vastly different trimming/shoeing needs. Because of the many variables, the only way to predict the perfect shoeing or trimming interval for a horse is direct experience. We can, however, make some general statements about hoof growth. On average a hoof grows between 3 1/4 and 4 inches annually. This means the hoof wall that is immediately below the coronary band today will be at ground level in about one year. A shod horse is usually due to be reset after 3/8 to 1/2 inch of hoof growth. With a little arithmetic we can establish an interval range.

A fast-growing horse that needs a reset with 3/8 (0.375) inch of growth:

4 inches/year ÷ 52 weeks/year
= 0.077 inch/week

0.375 inch of growth ÷ 0.077 inches week
= **4.87 weeks.**

A slow-growing horse that can handle a full 1/2 (0.5) inch of new growth:

3.25 inches/year ÷ 52 weeks/year
= 0.0625 inches/week

0.5 inch of growth ÷ 0.0625 inch/week
= **8 weeks.**

Now we have a range that tells us, in general, that a shod horse should be reset every five to eight weeks. To narrow this down further requires looking at each horse individually.

A shoe will protect the hoof wall well enough to completely eliminate wear. Shod feet will keep getting longer while a shoe is in place. For this reason one of the signals of excessive time between resets is stumbling. Overlong shoeing intervals can cause a horse to stumble in several ways. Getting long footed can cause a horse to feel uncertain on its feet, since simply having the extra length will increase the chances of a fall. More frequently, though, stumbling has to do with a low hoof angle and difficult breakover—the action of the hoof pivoting over the point of the toe as it leaves the ground (fig. 3.3). When the shoeing interval is too long, it is common for the heels of the overgrown hoof to spread beyond the edges of the shoe. When about half the thickness of the wall spreads this way, what is left on the shoe can no longer support the animal's weight, and the heels get crushed. At the same time, the toe continues to grow longer. This combination results in a quick lowering of the hoof angle in relation to the ground (fig. 3.4). A low angle causes difficult and slow breakover, resulting in a longer, lower stride. Stumbling occurs when the flatter arc of movement causes the long toe to meet the ground before the stride is complete. The picture gets more complicated because the angles on all the hooves rarely change at the same rate. This will cause the horse to have strides of differing lengths and heights—uncomfortable not only for the rider but for the horse as well.

It is best not to wait for these symptoms as a reminder to call the shoer, especially since it may be weeks until the appointment date. There are better indications of what shoeing interval is best for a horse.

Ideally, the quality of movement and the

**Figure 3.3** This series of drawings represents the action of breakover. Note that the toe penetrates the ground when possible.

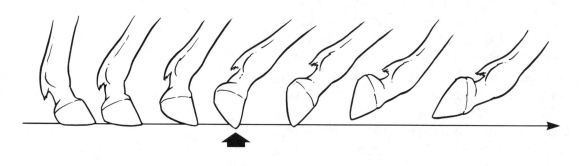

animal's comfort should be important factors in scheduling the farrier's visits. Stumbling is an extreme example, but more subtle changes can signal a need for the shoer's attention. Comfort, ease of motion, surefootedness, animation, and confidence are qualities that horses naturally possess to varying degrees. The test will be to notice changes and connect them to changes in the horse's feet. Being able to recognize balance and imbalance (chap. 5) will go a long way to help you identify a horse's hoof care needs. With this information, shoeing can be scheduled before a decline in performance occurs.

**Figure 3.4** (left) The heel has overgrown the shoe, causing weight to be supported by the inside half of the hoof wall at the heels. The inside half is crushed by the load, and the shoe becomes embedded in the foot. (right) A low hoof angle and a long toe results.

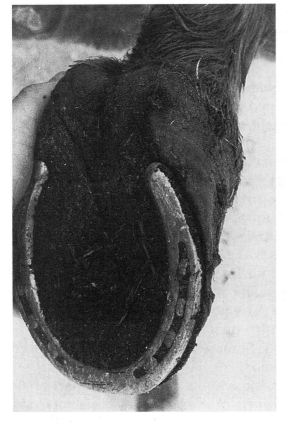
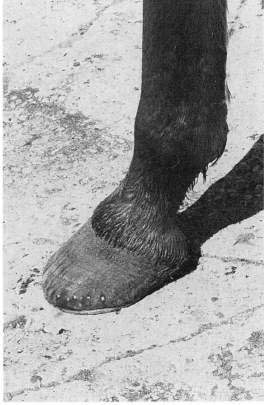

**ADDITIONAL FACTORS** Assessing the condition of a horse's feet is an ongoing task and it is an important habit to develop. Checking feet can easily be done at the same time as hooves are picked out. Tug on each shoe to be sure it is tight. Make sure the heels of the shoe are not bent down away from the hoof and that the nail clinches are still flat against the hoof wall. Watch for the development of serious cracks. Make sure the nails are in place. Check to see if a shoe has worn so thin that it has cracked or if the nailheads have worn small enough to pull through the nail holes. Much can be learned from a quick review of each hoof. If something doesn't seem right, maybe it can wait, or maybe rescheduling would be wise. Calling the farrier with an accurate description of the circumstances is a good way to share the responsibility of making these judgments.

**CAST SHOES** Horseshoes don't just fall off. They are stepped off, pried off, or sucked off. A shoe is stepped off when another foot holds it down while the foot itself is picked up; it may be pried off when hooked on a fence and jerked; or it may be sucked off when the nails are constantly worked at as the animal moves around in a muddy environment. Another variation of working at the nails is the horse that stamps all day on a hard surface to dislodge flies. These mishaps can occur even to an expertly applied shoe. The point is that steel nails do not spontaneously release, allowing the shoe to fly off. Something must happen to loosen the shoe.

The occasional cast shoe is a part of life for owners of shod horses. This is not to say that the horseshoer is never at fault, only that the horse is an accomplice. Recently a horse I work on lost a front shoe. The owner decided that since she wasn't riding she might as well pull the mate and let the horse go barefoot. She thought this would be easy, since the other had simply "fallen off " and she had the right tools. Three people and three hours later the shoe finally came off, and she had a comical story to tell about their efforts. I'm sure the horse had some stories of its own.

Shoes will be cast; the question is what to do when it happens. If the horse has tough, healthy feet and is shod only for long, rocky trail rides, scheduling a visit from the shoer may be all that is needed. If it is close to reset time, an easy ride on soft footing is permissible. Even if the hoof wears down a little, it will be trimmed anyway, and its mate will be trimmed to match. Generally, the hoof length difference caused by a missing shoe should not create problems during light relaxing work of short duration on good footing. However, if the missing shoe was designed to control a damaging gait defect, or had thick pads, creating a substantial length difference from its mate, good judgment must be used. Furthermore, if the next scheduled shoeing is weeks away or your horse has fragile feet, riding is not advisable. The best thing to do is to stall the horse and put on a hoof boot or wrap the foot with duct tape to protect the wall (fig. 3.5). This precaution will ensure that as much hoof as possible remains, so that the shoer need only nail on a replacement. If a lot of hoof has worn down or broken off, it may be necessary to reset the mate in order to maintain balanced movement. A little duct tape goes a long way. When in doubt, ask your farrier.

If you find a nail missing or dangling but the shoe is still tight, there is probably no cause for alarm. Under normal conditions, four nails are capable of securing a shoe, although six, seven, or eight are commonly used. If the nail is sticking straight out toward the other leg, however, it is wise to clip it off for safety. Many tools will work for this, including a bolt cutter or a side cutter. If these are not available, carefully bend the nail straight down with a hammer.

A shoe with a heel bent away from the hoof (sprung) more than 1/4 inch should be repaired at the shoer's first opportunity (fig. 3.6). A bent heel causes an immediate imbalance and is likely to be stepped on or hooked again. The other heel then bears an

**Figure 3.5** Duct tape is wrapped around the edge of a hoof with a missing shoe, helping to protect the hoof wall until the shoe can be replaced.

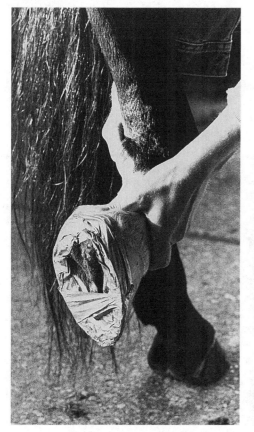

**Figure 3.6** The heel got hooked on a fence wire, but the horse pulled free before the shoe came off.

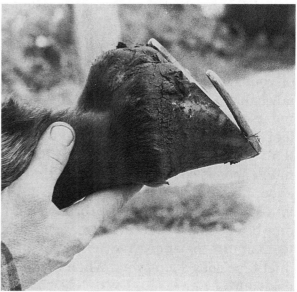

undue share of the weight, which can contribute to a condition called sheared heels (see chap. 7). Lesser bends, though not as serious, should still be brought to the shoer's attention.

Another problem that can arise between shoeings is loose shoes. How important immediate action is depends on how loose the shoe becomes. A shoe that can be wiggled slightly with strong hand pressure is technically loose. Depending on use and ground conditions, it may stay in place for weeks. The condition should be reported to the shoer, and described accurately so the appropriate scheduling decision can be made. If a reset is imminent and riding will not be excessive, nothing need be done until the scheduled appointment.

Consider however, what will happen if the loose shoe is cast: How well will the horse hold up? What about riding? Will the horse be pastured, making an expensive hand-forged shoe impossible to find? These are some of the questions that will play a part in deciding what action to take. If the shoe is very loose and easy to wiggle, it probably won't stay on long, and decisions can be made accordingly. Many changes can happen to a shoeing job that do not require immediate attention. But, if the horse is hobbling around on three shoes, one of them dangling by two nails, the perfectly planned 6 1/2-week interval becomes meaningless. Cooperative, common-sense interaction between owner and shoer will go a long way to help keep the horse sound and avoid costly, unnecessary visits from the shoer.

**DOING IT YOURSELF** I do not recommend learning how to do any part of the shoeing operation out of a book. But, I have yet to find a horseshoer who was unwilling to spend a few minutes instructing a customer on a couple of basic procedures. It is in the farrier's own best interest —if the owner can tighten a shoe, then the shoer need not make a special trip to do it.

It can be a great advantage to learn how to tighten as well as pull shoes. Both require only very basic tools and are fairly easy to learn. An investment of as little as $60 will buy a set of pull-offs, a shoeing hammer, a rasp, and a clincher (fig. 3.7), which is all you need to tighten or pull a shoe. At this price the tools will be of

**Figure 3.7** The tools used to tighten or pull a shoe: (left to right) shoeing hammer, pull-offs, clincher, and hoof rasp.

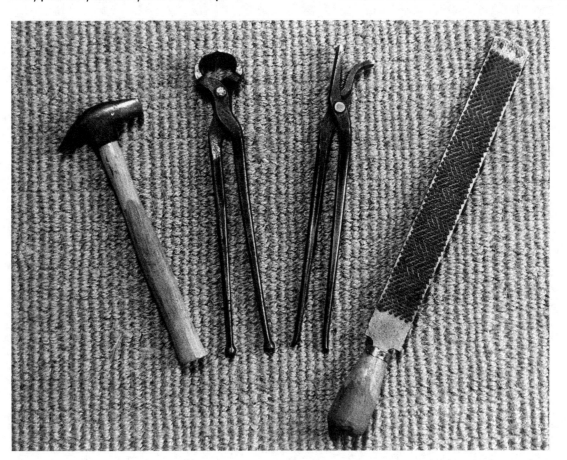

acceptable quality and serviceable enough for general use. Comparable tools of top quality designed for professional use could easily cost about $200, an unnecessary expenditure for the average horse owner.

Basic tightening is appropriate only when the shoe is not excessively loose; otherwise it may require some new nails. I do not recommend that owners pull shoes just to allow a horse to go barefoot. To do this correctly, the hooves should also be trimmed. Trimming is discussed in detail in chapter 5.

Being able to pull a shoe will be of great help, however, when the shoe is dangling or very loose. At these times there is danger that the horse will step on the exposed nails or damage the hoof wall if the shoe is twisted off.

In general it is wise not to be completely dependent on a shoer, particularly in an emergency, such as when you are about to enter the ring or start a trail ride and hear the characteristic sound of a loose shoe.

## TRIMMING INTERVALS

A horse that has tough, healthy feet and is not ridden a lot can often get along fine without shoes, but stone bruises and tender feet are more likely to be problems for barefoot horses. The front feet are particularly susceptible, since more weight is carried in front and the soles tend to be flatter than those of the hind feet. Anytime a horse is limping or acts sore-footed, the cause should be determined. A horse whose hooves have simply worn so short that walking (especially on gravel), causes uncomfortable pressure on the soles will show immediate improvement when shod.

Calculating a schedule for trimming an unshod horse is done by the same basic criteria as for shoeing, with one major exception. Owners do not have the luxury of knowing for certain that the interval will fall between five and eight weeks. If the hooves wear evenly and at about the same rate as they grow, trims can safely be at much longer intervals, though lateral balance, angle, length, and general condition will still need to be tracked. Alternatively, some animals will require very frequent care to maintain balance. In these cases shoes can stop the uneven wear and extend the interval. Most unshod horses, however, fall into a trimming cycle similar to that for shod animals. Their hooves begin getting long or out of balance at about the same time as the shod horses need a reset. Again, the primary consideration should be the horse's comfort and ease of movement.

Even if the horse requires only minimal hoof care, it is prudent to have the shoer visit periodically. This practice will confirm your own assessment of the hooves and keep the animal in the habit of standing for the farrier. Problems can be averted before they become serious, and you will already have a relationship with a shoer when shoes are needed for a long trail ride or an upcoming show.

Once the proper shoeing/trimming interval is determined, it may be difficult to integrate this information with real-life scheduling factors. Owning two or more horses with different needs can complicate this even more. These problems are minimized if the horses are boarded at a big barn where the shoer visits frequently. Each animal can have its own schedule. And, if there are enough horses or if neighbors can coordinate their efforts, perhaps the horses can be split into two groups—for example, a six-week group and a seven-week group. Otherwise compromises will have to be made. Often the horse with the shortest interval or greatest care requirements will dictate all the others' scheduling. In any case, decisions will have to be made that take into account fairness to the horses, the availability of the shoer, and the owner's financial and scheduling concerns. With a little experimentation and some record keeping, a convenient system can be devised.

The time to start thinking about straight and conformationally correct limbs is when you decide which horses should be bred. Crooked limbs are commonly passed on from one or both parents. The next best time is before you buy a horse. It costs the same amount to feed—and less to maintain—a high-quality, well-built horse as a poorly conformed one that will eventually need extra care. If you choose carefully, you can avoid many disappointments. There are books to help with this, as well as local resources like an equine veterinarian.

An investment in proper hoof care for a young horse will pay dividends for the rest of its life. It is true to some extent that, while a horse is very young, conformational flaws can be improved by proper trimming. Until the horse is about nine months old, the development of the bones of the legs can be both positively and negatively affected by the balance of the feet. In fact, conformation problems can actually be created by lax care. Avoiding or correcting this type of environmentally caused defect is more likely

## WHEN TO START YOUNGSTERS

than compensating for a genetic flaw, although some genetically induced problems can be improved on. In either case, the chances for improvement are very poor once the bones stop growing.

At any rate, it is much easier to keep a horse straight than to straighten it. It requires months of work before the growth plates of the bones close to have any chance of improving conformation (chap. 2 discusses bone development and growth plates). A foal should have its first farrier visit at about one month, and never past three months. The horse then has the best opportunity to grow straight, and as little as possible is left to luck.

Balanced trimming is all most young horses need. Corrective trimming of youngsters refers to purposely trimming the hooves out of balance. By correction I mean inducing permanent changes that do not need constant reinforcement to be maintained. This practice shifts weight distribution and alters the alignment of joints, thus affecting bone growth. It is a very serious undertaking that requires skill, knowledge, intuition, and experience, and even then there is no guarantee of success. There is a lot of controversy regarding correcting conformation flaws in horses. Several points though, seem to be universally accepted:

- The younger the horse is when started, the better the results will be.
- Trying to improve conformation in a horse beyond nine months old almost never works. The long-term result of attempting change in a more mature horse is usually deformed feet and eventual lameness.

- Any purposeful hoof imbalance created to improve conformation, stance, or gait must be done graduallyand with great care.
- Excessive lateral balance changes cause lameness.
- To be effective, frequent trimming (no less often than once a month) is necessary until the change is stabilized and the growth plates have closed. Otherwise natural hoof growth and wear will undo any gains.
- The odds of success decrease the farther up the leg the flaw is situated.

Before the first exciting farrier visit, the foal must learn to wear a halter, be led, and be restrained. It should also have some experience with having its feet touched and picked up. Fortunately, these lessons are easier and safer to teach when the animal weighs two hundred pounds rather than a few months later at five hundred pounds.

# 4

---

# Preparing for
# the Shoer

A successful shoeing program requires a cooperative effort between owner, shoer, and horse. The owner provides the work environment and a horse that is ready to be worked on. The shoer brings the equipment and the skills needed to complete the job correctly. On the horse's part, a willing attitude allows the procedure to move pleasantly and efficiently. If all the participants know and take responsibility for their roles, having a horse shod goes quickly and the horse gets the best possible care. When any part of the picture is missing, problems will always arise.

One of the basic lessons horses must learn is to stand quietly and allow humans to touch and handle them. This includes permitting someone to open their mouths, look in their ears, and pick up and hold their feet. Unless a horse learns to accept this, every time it is groomed or every time a veterinarian or shoer visits it will become an ordeal for everyone involved. If the problem is bad enough, it can be such a nuisance that it even overshadows an animal's great athletic ability.

Few animals are born willing to be handled in this way. They must be taught. This responsibility rests on the owner, not the horseshoer. It is a mistake to assume that a shoer is also a horse trainer. These two professions require very different skills as well as different equipment. Although some shoers have a great deal of skill as trainers and may even derive a portion of their income from training, most do not. Nevertheless, out of necessity, many shoers have learned techniques to convince horses to stand still to be trimmed and shod. Yet this is not the same as being a trainer. The difference is simple enough: the goal of a trainer is to educate the horse and cause long-term modification of its behavior; the goal of a shoer is to trim a horse and put shoes on. When it comes to getting shoes on an uncooperative animal, shoers are not thinking about long-term training needs; they are thinking about getting done as quickly as possible without being hurt.

Most people assume that the main risk to a horseshoer is getting kicked. Although being kicked by a hind foot certainly can be damaging, a shoer is more at risk of being bitten or struck with a front foot. One of the dangers is being cut by a nail that has just

## DISCIPLINE AND PROPER BEHAVIOR

been driven and is sticking out the side of the hoof. If the horse picks this moment to jerk its foot away, the shoer stands the chance of being seriously hurt. It is easy to understand why having horses properly trained and disciplined is so important to a professional horseshoer.

An owner should set aside time to work with the horse. Holding the foot up for a few moments and then setting it down is a simple but effective beginning upon which all other lessons can be built. The foot can then be held up longer and cleaned out with a hoof pick. One should also practice holding the foot up and tapping it with the round side of the pick so that the horse learns to keep its balance during shoeing and not fear the sound of the hammer. The main lesson the horse must learn is that the decision to put a foot down is made by the person, not the horse.

In general, the basic lessons should be worked out before the shoer arrives. If the owner cannnot deal with behavior problems, the services of a professional trainer should be enlisted. This is not to say that shoers never teach a horse to stand properly. All too often they must do this in order to get along with the animal and get paid for completing the shoeing job. But it is safer and more responsible on the part of the owner to teach the horse the lesson before it is expected to cooperate for an hour. Furthermore, it is not wise to assume that a horseshoer on a tight work schedule has the time to teach a horse basic manners.

Any shoer understands that horses are not statues. Even the most cooperative animal may lean a little and wiggle around out of boredom or because it is bothered by flies. This is well within reasonable limits.

What is not acceptable is the horse that aggressively fights the shoer. There are, of course, other reasons why a horse may be uncooperative. It may be afraid or simply not understand what is expected. These circumstances require patience and guidance, not heavy-handed discipline. But uncooperative and dangerous behavior that is simply a bad habit or a struggle for dominance may require a firmer approach.

Owners should realize that, when forced to act as trainer, a shoer can't be expected to decide on methods compatible with those of the owner. To avoid bad feelings, it is advisable for owner and shoer to reach an agreement on how to deal with problems. There are many opinions on what is and is not a reasonable correction to impose on a horse. Some people believe it is never appropriate to strike a horse. While it is often not the only way to achieve results, done correctly it can be a quick and effective method of stopping undesirable behavior. Factors such as age, temperament, and the reasons for the horse's behavior should be considered before using this method. No matter what means of correction is chosen, it should not be used in anger. Deciding in advance what approach to take lets discipline be administered very quickly, so the horse will relate the behavior to the consequence without the risk that angry acts will lead to injury of horse or person. Any action that risks serious injury to the animal cannot be considered a normal or acceptable correction.

Even-tempered correction is an important key to encouraging a horse's cooperation. If the owner or shoer does not exert authority as herd leader, the horse will. Once established, this improper role reversal can only lead to trouble. This should not be misinterpreted to justify physical abuse. But by watching horses interact with each other it is easy to see that the lead animals use discipline (including kicking and biting) to maintain herd order. This is natural behavior for a horse and a form of communication that is clearly understood.

If a horse acts up in a way that makes it difficult or impossible (and dangerous) to complete the shoeing, the owner should be prepared for the shoer to take some corrective action. This may mean soothing a frightened animal, or for a stubborn, spoiled horse it could mean slapping the horse's belly with a hand or sometimes with the flat of a rasp. The belly is chosen because we puny humans can get the message across here, and there are no bony surfaces to injure. Hitting the belly, of course, would never be appropriate on a pregnant mare. If an owner has strong feelings about a particular method of discipline, the shoer should be informed beforehand. But the owner should be willing to offer an alternative way (that works) to get the horse to stand properly.

One method is distracting the animal, such as by tapping its forehead, or by using a training bridle, or a lead-shank chain across the nose, by holding an ear, or by using a twitch (fig. 4.1). Using a twitch can be dangerous, however, since on occasion a twitched horse will react violently without warning. Another method is tying up a hind leg with a rope arrangement called a sideline, making it impossible for the horse to put the foot on the ground (fig. 4.2). When this is done correctly, the horse quickly learns that to fight having a leg held up is a useless effort. In learning this, however, it is likely to struggle and fall several times. Experienced helpers and a large, safe working area are a must when using this approach. Sometimes the solution to problem behavior can be as simple as having another horse stand within sight or turning the animal around so it can see in another direction. When all else fails, it may be necessary to arrange for a veterinarian to administer a tranquilizer before the horse is to be shod. In many cases this works well when the dosage achieves a balance between relaxed and so drugged the animal cannot stand up. However, the people must not let their guard down because on rare occasions a sound or movement will shake a tranquilized horse from its relaxed state

**Figure 4.1** A twitch (left) and a training bridle (right). Each works well on some horses, depending on temperament. The bridle has the advantage of not imposing a correction when behavior is acceptable, much like the correct use of a choke collar to train a dog.

and it can become violent with little warning.

A common mistake, in my opinion, is to try to bribe a misbehaving horse with affection or food treats to convince it to cooperate. This will nearly always have the opposite effect from the one desired. If you give a treat or a kind gesture to a recalcitrant horse, the message is clear: "If I misbehave, I get rewarded." Positive reinforcement should be used only in response to behavior that you want the horse to repeat.

As a last resort, the shoer may tell the owner to put the horse away and call when it has been taught some basic manners. Some people are offended by this attitude, but they need to realize that to a self-

**Figure 4.2** A horse tied with a sideline, which prevents the foot from touching the ground. The animal learns that resisting is no use. This procedure can be dangerous and requires experienced help, since the horse is likely to struggle and fall. This is more in the realm of training than of horseshoeing.

employed person, getting injured on the job can be financially devastating. All horse-shoers have limits on the amount of risk they are willing to subject themselves to for the price of a shoeing job.

Nevertheless, the people involved should not forget that sometimes the horse is justified in resisting. For instance, a horse cannot be expected to lift a foot willingly and quietly if bearing weight on the other side causes a lot of pain. Biting flies can be a problem, and some shoers seem to hold up legs in a way that causes some horses to get muscle cramps. Common sense dictates that any of these circumstances can be remedied. If necessary, the cause of the pain should be diagnosed and treated. If shoeing is part of the treatment and the horse cannot withstand the discomfort, the pain can be alleviated at least temporarily by a veterinarian. Flies can be discouraged with a repellant, and the shoer can bend down farther or give the animal periodic breaks.

## THE RIGHT SETTING

The ideal spot for shoeing is a quiet, level, well-lit, safe place where the horse can be tied securely. The area should be large enough so the shoer can move freely around the animal and can stretch out its hind legs without being crammed against a wall. The work area should be well ventilated but shielded from harsh weather, including direct sunlight on hot days. It should also be possible to drive a work vehicle fairly near so that tools and equipment need not be carried long distances.

This sort of work area offers the safest, most relaxed atmosphere for both horse and shoer. It affords the best opportunity for the two to get along and complete the task as calmly and quickly as possible. Such conditions help shoers do their best work. Recognizing that a farrier's visits are an ongoing necessity of horse ownership, it is wise to take this into account when designing a barn.

Of primary importance are safety and lighting. If the weather is reasonable and a qualified person is available to hold the horse, these may be achieved in the driveway. Crossties in the barn aisle are often available and usually work well. Otherwise, existing facilities can be modified to an acceptable level. You can ask the horseshoer which area is most suitable or how to make some spot safe and usable.

## KEEPING A GOOD SHOER

Finding a shoer you have confidence in and then being told that person no longer has time to service your horse can be a very frustrating experience. But skilled professionals are always at a premium, and each can care for only a certain number of animals. Because consistent, high-quality work will always be in demand, good shoers frequently find themselves with more business than they can handle. The only solution is to stop working on some of the horses. Common sense dictates that these will be the accounts that are, for whatever reason, the least desirable. Some variables, such as how far away the barn is, are beyond the owner's control. Most, however, can be controlled to decrease the odds of being cut from a farrier's customer list.

Horseshoers want the same basic things out of their work that anyone wants. They want to perform their job safely under decent conditions, make a reasonable profit, and get paid promptly for their services. They want to be respected for skills that took years to learn and refine, and they want to see tangible results from their efforts. Any customer who provides these opportunities likewise deserves respect and appreciation and has done everything that could be reasonably expected to keep a good shoer. Here are some examples of situations that affect the shoer-customer relationship.

A horse that fights shoeing is a farrier's nightmare. The owner who isn't putting energy into resolving this problem is high on the list of customers to drop.

Another sure way to make that list is not to pay promptly. A bill should be considered due upon receipt and certainly always within ten days unless other arrangements have been made.

Horses that receive only intermittent care and are therefore trimmed or shod on very long cycles represent a special problem for shoers. These horses, with one missing shoe, different lengths and angles and hoof deformities, as well as cracks and chips, are substantially more work to shoe properly than one that is regularly maintained. Additionally, depending on how bad the feet are, correct angles and optimum length may not be possible. It can be very discouraging to work hard, invest half again as much time as usual, and still have a product that is not quite what it should be. Shoers are always trying to upgrade their clientele to people interested in providing their horses with consistent care.

One of the most difficult problems for an owner to overcome is not having enough horses to make the trip worthwhile for a busy shoer. Sometimes a trip charge can be negotiated to cover travel time. If not, the solution is for several neighbors with horses to be available at the same time. If all else fails, it is sometimes possible to bring the horse to a location where the shoer will be working.

An owner should understand that horseshoers are trying to balance more than just feet. They are also juggling a list of customers who have come to depend on their shoer. It may be impossible to drop everything and drive thirty miles to replace a missing shoe. The farrier should be given a couple of days to rearrange schedules to fit in a special trip, and a sporadic customer should not expect the same consideration.

The farrier should always be provided with a clean and functional working situation. Standing on the side of a hill, ankle-deep in mud or manure, or on a surface so bumpy that it's impossible to tell if the hoof angle matches the pastern makes doing a good job nearly impossible. Unable to do the job properly, a farrier may resent coming, and drop that location altogether.

Horses should be caught and either tied or stalled nearby before the shoer arrives to begin work. Shoers who must wait for someone to go catch the horses end up late to every other appointment for the rest of the day.

The horseshoer should not be expected to act as a groom. The animals should be cleaned up beforehand so that work can proceed without delay. If the horses are pastured, any mud should be cleaned off ahead of time. Furthermore, hoof dressing should not be applied within twenty-four hours of the shoer's arrival. These greasy substances get on hands, make tools hard to handle, and tend to gum them up.

An owner with a history of missed appointments should expect that eventually the appointments will be refused.

Most shoers appreciate the opportunity to wash up after completing their work at a barn so they can eat lunch with clean hands or be more comfortable while driving to their next stop.

To the owner, horses may simply be a recreational or part-time pursuit, but to shoers they are an intrinsic part of their work, a way to earn a living. An owner may not mind a few hours each week of standing in mud or working in dirty conditions; but when a task goes on eight to ten hours a day, six days a week, the circumstances and conditions take on great importance. We all respond positively and do a better job when we are treated with respect and provided with pleasant, functional working conditions.

In return, owners should be treated respectfully. They should not have to take time off from work only to be left standing around, waiting hours for the shoer to arrive. Shoeing options should be explained, problems should be identified, and their questions warrant answers. Most important, their horses deserve consistently good care by a responsible, nonabusive professional.

There is nothing better than a relationship between owner and shoer that is based on mutual respect, each being considerate of the other's needs. In these cases everybody wins: the horses get the best possible care, and the farrier's visits become another interesting and enjoyable part of horse ownership.

# 5

## Sizing up a trim

Trimming entails cutting away excess hoof growth (like trimming our own fingernails). It also involves sculpting the hoof to correct any deformities and either rounding the edges to avoid chipping on an unshod hoof or preparing the foot to receive a shoe. It is the most exacting part of horseshoeing. A good trim is paramount in achieving a good shoeing job because it is the foundation for the entire operation. This point is clearly demonstrated in that shortening the toe by only a quarter of an inch will raise the hoof angle in relation to the ground by as much as three degrees.

A quarter inch taken at the heels will lower the angle. A difference of a quarter inch on either side of the hoof will determine whether the hoof lands squarely during movement.

Taken together, the hoof angle and side-to-side symmetry of each hoof represent how well balanced the animal is in relation to the conformation of its legs. Balance affects not only the position of the hoof and how it lands but, more significantly, the position of the bones inside. By influencing the dynamic forces applied to the ligaments, tendons, and joints, the alignment of the bones of the hoof and leg controls how the stress of weight bearing and movement is distributed. Ultimately, the entire weight-bearing and concussion-absorbing mechanism is directly affected by the trim. As a result, any long-standing imbalance caused by poor trimming, uneven wear of an unshod hoof, or excessively long shoeing intervals can cause or contribute to a variety of problems such as splints, navicular disease, and sheared heels (see chap. 7).

Some problems can develop or be exacerbated as soon as an imbalance is present. For example, toeing in or toeing out as well as gait abnormalities such as stumbling and overreaching can be caused by hoof imbalance. When balance is restored, these problems are resolved. If tendons were strained because of an unnatural hoof position, however, some time may be needed for the horse to recover completely.

In addition, imbalance can lead to distorted hoof growth in the form of flares and dishes (figs. 5.1 and 5.2). These deformities adversely affect the shock-absorbing qualities of the hoof, weaken a portion of the hoof wall, and can change the breakover point.

**Figure 5.1** A flared hoof.

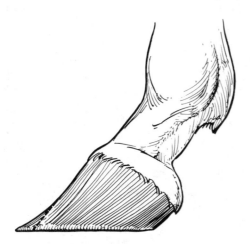

**Figure 5.2** A dished hoof.

The results of poor balance are many and varied; at the least, the horse will not move with confidence and comfort.

When trimming a horse, a conscientious shoer will appraise many factors to determine whether a state of balance has been achieved. When a horse is properly balanced, the angle of the hoof wall, as viewed from the side, will match the angle of the bones of the pastern; viewed from the front, the bones of the leg create a straight line perpendicular to the ground and centered above the hoof; the coronary band will be parallel to the ground; the bulbs of the heels will be an equal distance from the ground; the hoof shape, as viewed from the top and bottom, will be symmetrical, and each hoof will match its mate in these aspects, including overall length. In addition, when the horse is moving, each hoof should land squarely, so that one side of a hoof does not touch the ground before the other side. Each of these conditions can be met every time a trim is properly performed on a horse with healthy feet and excellent conformation.

However, balance has to be viewed in relation to what nature has provided each animal. Sometimes meeting one of the criteria above will make it impossible to meet another. For instance, a shoer may find that if the hoof is trimmed so that the coronary band is parallel to the ground, the leg bones are not centered above the hoof. If the hoof is trimmed so that the bony column is centered, the shoer may well discover that not only is the coronary band not level, but the hoof no longer lands squarely during movement. These types of problems reflect conformation flaws in the horse.

When approaching a horse with conformation problems, the goal is to match nature's intent as closely as possible for that particular animal. This results in a comfortable horse with the least possible strain on its internal structures: a state of balance. It takes practice to develop "an eye" for when balance exists (and when it doesn't). Gaining this skill begins with learning to recognize balance in a well-conformed horse, as described above. This applies to both horseshoers and owners. Ensuring proper balance is certainly important enough to warrant the effort.

Following is a discussion of the five components of a good trim. The descriptions are in general based on how each aspect looks on a well-conformed animal with healthy feet. When judging a trim one must take into account what the horseshoer had to start with. If a horse has severely worn down or crushed heels, for instance, it may not be possible to trim the feet on an ideal angle. No one can magically grow hoof wall or make cracks disappear. Flared feet and other deformities may take several shoeings to correct.

## HOOF ANGLE

The hoof angle refers to the angle of the hoof in relation to the ground surface. Many people attempt to assign a specific angle, measured in degrees, to all horses in general or to horses of a particular breed or specialized use. Even some books claim that a certain measurement is the "ideal" angle. But not all horses are built to the same specifications, so this seems to me about as sensible as assuming that all people of a certain ancestry wear an 8 1/2 D shoe.

The ideal hoof angle for comfort and

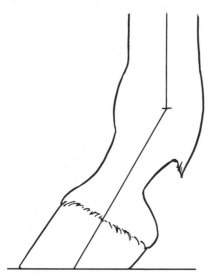

**Figure 5.3** Correct hoof angle.

**Figure 5.4** A correct hoof angle will match the pastern angle, which is the same as the angle of the shoulder blade.

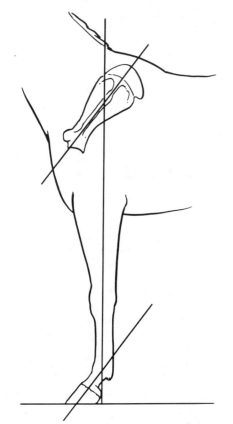

proper function is basically the same as the pastern angle (fig. 5.3). It will generally fall within a certain range (45-60 degrees) but cannot be correctly determined without considering the individual horse. Properly matching a front hoof to its pastern will also match it to the angle of the shoulder (fig. 5.4). Limited only by conformation, this allows efficient and harmonious functioning of the entire limb. Finally, unless there is a defect or deformity, the two front feet will match and the two hind feet will match. Occasionally the front and hind feet will all naturally be at the same angle.

Matching a hoof to its mate primarily involves using a practiced eye to see that the first hoof of the pair has been trimmed to an acceptable angle. The hoof is then measured with a hoof protractor (fig. 5.5). Using this measurement as a guide, the mate is trimmed to match. Angle measurements can also be taken with a tape measure or a caliper, because if the length of the toes match and the length of the heels match, the angles must be the same. That the numbers arrived at by various measuring gauges and techniques do not always totally agree from one shoer to another is unimportant. What is important is that the angles suit the animal and that each method show the paired feet to be the same.

To judge this portion of a trim, the horse must be inspected while standing squarely on a flat, level surface. The viewer should stand back from the horse and kneel down slightly while looking at the lower leg from the side (fig. 5.6). The right hoof is judged from the right side and the left from the left side. Notice that in figure 5.3 the hoof line is parallel to the pastern bones, not the front edge of the pastern. Figure 5.7 offers

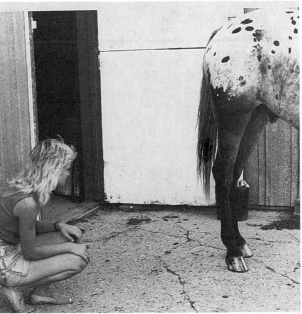

**Figure 5.6** Sighting a hind foot to check hoof angle.

**Figure 5.5** A hoof protractor, often called a hoof gauge, measures the angle of the hoof in degrees.

**Figure 5.7** (left) A hoof angle steeper (more upright) than the pastern angle; (right) a hoof angle lower than the pastern angle.

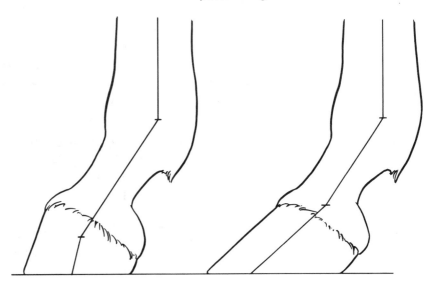

an idea of what incorrect angles can look like. If both feet appear suited to their pasterns, their angles will naturally be matched to each other as well. Using this method, with practice you can identify a variation from one hoof to its mate of less than two degrees.

## LATERAL BALANCE

To be balanced laterally (from side to side), both sides of the hoof should be equal in length, as should the heels. With good conformation, the hoof will then be centered beneath the bones of the leg, and the foot will land squarely during movement. This aspect of trimming is the most difficult to judge correctly, and poor conformation complicates the picture, making evaluation even more difficult.

If one side of the hoof is longer, it will land first. The traction on one side only causes the foot to pivot at the initial point of contact. Generally the pivot is in the direction of the longer side. Therefore if the outside wall is longer than the inside wall, the horse will tend to toe out on landing. The reverse is also true. In both cases, the breakover point is altered, causing a modified flight pattern.

When done with discretion, purposely leaving one side longer may help a horse with certain gait problems: done excessively, it will cause lameness. It is my opinion, however, that with few exceptions each horse should be trimmed to be as balanced as possible. At this point any essential gait alteration can be made with corrective shoes.

There is often a temptation to use the balance of a hoof to give a poorly conformed leg the appearance of straightness. There are many long-term risks to this practice: the alignment of the bones has to be the guide.

In observing lateral balance, the horse must still be standing squarely on a level surface. The leg being judged should be looked at head-on. In other words, if the horse toes out the viewer should be somewhat to the side; if the leg is square with the horse, directly in front. Imagine that the limb being examined is a cord and that the hoof is hanging freely at the bottom. If it is indeed balanced, the hoof will look as if gravity is holding it symmetrically below the leg (fig. 5.8). If the hoof leans to one side, chances are good that an ideal condition of balance does not exist (fig. 5.9).

**Figure 5.8** (left) A laterally balanced foot. The leg is centered over the hoof. Notice that the chalk line points straight up the leg.

**Figure 5.9** (right) A laterally unbalanced hoof. This is the same leg pictured in figure 5.8 before the foot was trimmed correctly. The leg is not centered above the hoof, which appears to lean toward the outside. In this case the medial (inside, toward the midline of the animal) side of the hoof is shorter than the outside wall. Note that the chalk line, which follows the hoof horn tubules, points toward the inside of the leg instead of straight up the leg.

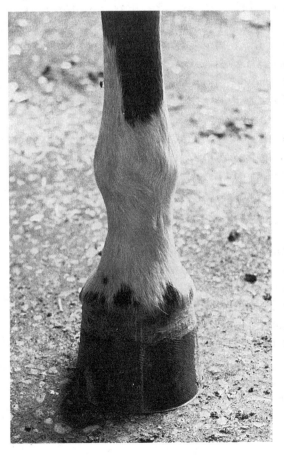

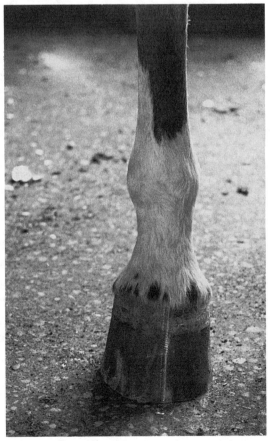

A further check of lateral balance can be accomplished by sighting the foot while holding it up. Ideally, the bottom plane of the hoof should be perpendicular to the leg (fig. 5.10). In a well-conformed horse it will also be perpendicular to the midline of the body. By looking down from exactly above the hoof and aligning your vision across the plane of the hoof's bottom surface, you can see if the two sides of a hoof are the same length.

When sighting a hoof in this fashion it is imperative that the leg be held gently at the bottom of the cannon bone of the front leg and beneath the hock of the hind leg, not at the pastern or the hoof itself, and in the position most natural to the horse (fig. 5.11). The leg and hoof must hang in a relaxed manner and must not be pulled out away from the body or held in a way that alters the position of the hoof. Anything else will provide faulty information.

Remember that even a perfect state of hoof balance will not eliminate conformation flaws. For instance, achieving balance will not straighten a cow-hocked horse, it will simply make it a more comfortable, more efficient cow-hocked horse.

## SHAPING THE HOOF

Shaping a hoof, called "dressing down the hoof," simply means rasping away distorted hoof growth, such as flares, dishes, and other hoof irregularities. These types of deformities, particularly flares, are often a symptom of a long-standing lateral imbalance and should not be considered a mere cosmetic problem. An asymmetrical hoof shape will cause many changes in the horse's form and function.

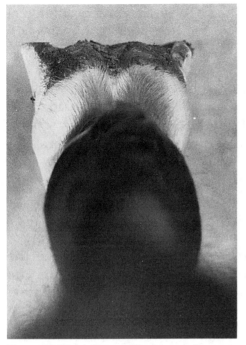

**Figure 5.10** (above) The view when sighting a hind hoof as shown in figure 5.11. The leg hangs in its most relaxed and natural position as the viewer looks over the hock to align her vision with the plane of the bottom of the hoof. In this way it can be seen if the bottom of the hoof is perpendicular to the bones of the lower leg. The animal's conformation must be considered.

**Figure 5.11** (above right) Correct method of sighting a front foot. Note that the hoof and leg are permitted to hang freely and the viewer moves to look directly over the bottom plane of the hoof. (right) Correct method of sighting a hind foot. The hoof and leg again hang freely, and the viewer looks directly over the bottom plane of the hoof.

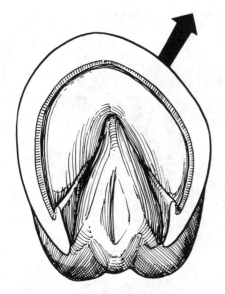

**Figure 5.12** If the shape of the hoof is irregular, the breakover will take the course of least resistance (in this case, the direction the arrow points) and alter the flight pattern of the leg.

For instance, a hump on the outside of the toe area will lever the horse's weight back to the inside heel and change the point at which the foot breaks over (fig. 5.12). The inside heel will usually break down from this extra stress, making the inside wall shorter than the outside wall. This sets up the chain of events common to lateral imbalance. Dishes and flares will also interfere with the normal expansion and contraction of the hoof, lessen its shock-absorbing qualities, and make the horse more susceptible to concussion-related lameness.

If hoof deformities are present, part of the trimming process should include taking the foot forward and using a rasp to create a more symmetrical hoof shape (fig. 5.13), whether the horse is to be shod or not. By

**Figure 5.13** With the hoof resting either on the shoer's knee or, as in this case, on a hoof stand, flares, dishes, and other irregularities are removed with a hoof rasp.

maintaining balance over a period of time, including shaping the deformed hoof, the problem can often be permanently resolved.

When a horse is to be left unshod, the edge of the hoof wall should be filed all around to remove sharpness. Beveling the hoof in this way reduces chipping of the wall and lessens the risk that a sharp edge will cut a person picking up a freshly trimmed hoof.

It is important that the shoe not put pressure on the sole of the horse's foot. Constant pressure on the sole will cause bruising and can eventually kill some of the sensitive living sole inside the hoof. If this tissue dies an abscess will form, and infection and lameness are not far behind. The abscess must be cut open to drain and the foot soaked in a strong solution of Epsom salts in warm water. To avoid this problem, the sole is trimmed so that the hoof wall alone bears the pressure of the shoe (fig. 5.14). A space only the thickness of a matchbook between the shoe and the sole is sufficient (fig. 5.15). Paring the sole also exposes the hoof wall to permit its trimming and gives the shoer a good look at the underlying tissue. This is an opportunity to identify problems such as bruises or punctures.

There are several schools of thought regarding what to do with the frog. Some shoers like to trim it even with the trimmed hoof wall or just short enough so it is not the first thing to hit the ground. This is usually enough to uncover any underlying problems (such as thrush or a puncture wound), and because the foot sinks into the ground, the frog will still bear weight as it should.

## TRIMMING THE SOLE AND FROG

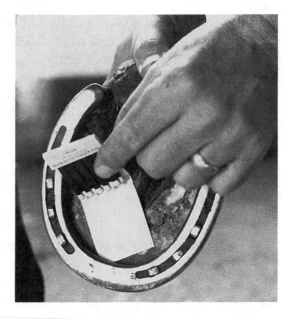

**Figure 5.14** The sole is trimmed to avoid pressure from the shoe, expose the excess hoof wall for trimming, and determine if any underlying problems exist.

**Figure 5.15** (above right) Leaving even a very small space between the sole and the shoe will avoid any risk of causing a bruise or an abscess.

The sides of the frog are also trimmed to make it easier to clean out the commissures (crevices), and ragged, dangling pieces are removed to keep them from tearing (fig. 5.16). Other farriers will trim much more—I presume to keep the frog farther from the ground and protect it from bruising, for cosmetic reasons, or to make certain there are no hidden problems. Still others hardly touch the frog at all, allowing it to bear as much weight as possible. All three approaches can be defended; in my opinion, however, the moderate approach of conservative trimming allows weight bearing while still permitting an adequate inspection. Where thrush is a problem, it is necessary to remove as much of the affected tissue as possible (see chap. 7).

**OVERALL HOOF LENGTH** The terrain and the use the horse is put to should be considered when determining how much hoof will be removed during trimming, but at any rate the front feet

**(a)**

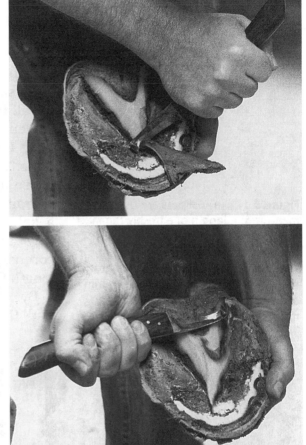

**(b)**

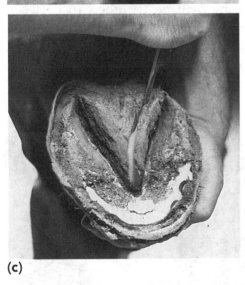

**(c)**

**(d)**

**Figure 5.16** (a) An untrimmed frog. (b, c) The sides are trimmed to allow easy cleaning with a hoof pick and to encourage debris to fall out on its own. (d) The frog is being trimmed approximately even with the level the hoof wall will be at after trimming. (e) Frog trimming is complete.

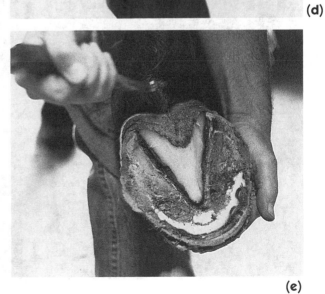

**(e)**

should be of equal length, as should the hind feet (fig. 5.17). If a horse is to go barefoot, the hoof is generally left a little longer than for shoeing, which increases traction and offers more protection for an unshod foot.

No single hoof length can be established for all horses, because hoof length is controlled by the distance between the coronary band and the bottom of the coffin bone. This distance will vary from horse to horse and is determined by heredity. On average however, measured at the toe area, a light horse will be trimmed to between 3 1/4 and 4 inches of hoof length from the coronary band to the ground, allowing more length for draft horses and less for ponies.

By observing texture and appearance and the resistance of the sole to finger

**Figure 5.17** (a) Calipers are used to measure the length of a freshly trimmed hoof. (b) Without changing the space between the arms of the calipers, the shoer marks the untrimmed hoof at the toe to identify how much hoof to trim away to match its previously trimmed mate. A tape measure can also be used.

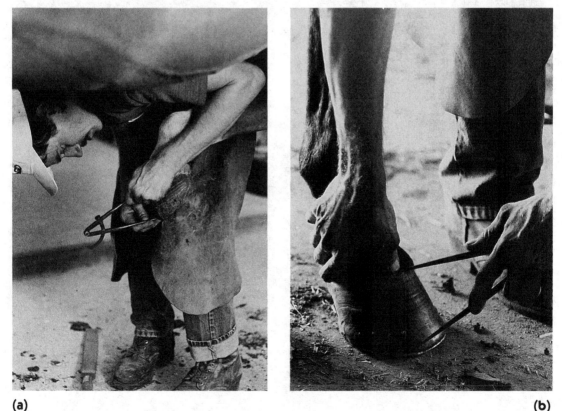

(a)

(b)

pressure, a shoer can tell when the hoof is as short as it can safely be trimmed. Sole material that has been dead tissue for a longer period (and is therefore farther from living tissue) has a dry, chalky, grainy, or flaky appearance and feel. As this tissue is pared away with a hoof knife to permit trimming the wall (fig. 5.18), the farrier eventually reaches smooth and resilient dead sole material. This is an indication that living tissue is not far away.

At the point where the sole becomes very soft and therefore gives easily to finger pressure, there is only about 1/16 to 1/8 inch of dead sole covering the living tissue. Such an animal has been trimmed too short and will probably be tenderfooted for a few days after shoeing. Occasionally this can be hard to avoid, since the layers of sole material can vary in thickness, making it difficult to gauge. Should this thin covering be trimmed away with the hoof knife, blood will flow. Though such close trimming is obviously not advisable, the blood can be stopped by cauterizing the cut with a piece of steel heated in the forge. This relatively painless procedure kills any bacteria and seals the wound. No long-term problems should result.

In general, you can expect a horse to go six to eight weeks between shoeings. If by three or four weeks the animal starts stumbling, the hooves overrun the shoes at the heels, or the angles become noticeably lower (long toe, low heels), it may be that more hoof should have been removed. Other possibilities are that the animal was trimmed at too low an angle or that the shoes were not fitted properly (see chap. 6).

In some cases, for specific reasons, horses are kept near a certain length. For example,

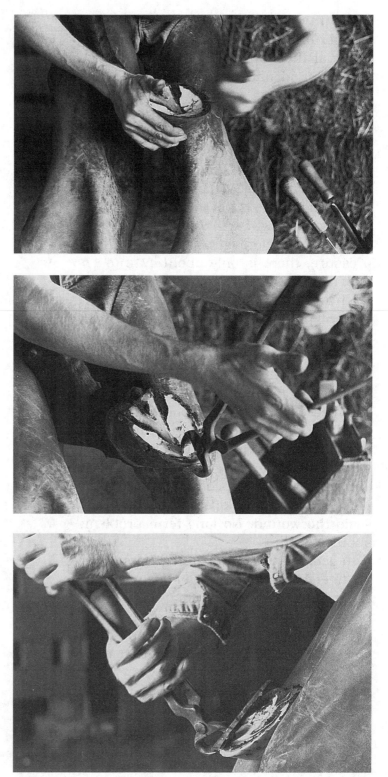

**Figure 5.18** Once the sole is trimmed, the exposed excess hoof wall can easily be trimmed with hoof nippers.

to avoid show disqualification, Arabian horses must not exceed 4 1/2 inches of hoof length from the hairline to the ground (including a shoe). Because a longer foot encourages these animals to move in their characteristic animated way, owners often prefer to keep the hoof length as close to the limit as possible. The horse must be shod more often to keep the hooves within this small range. Similarly, some racehorses are shod frequently to keep the hooves as short and light as possible.

A fair and accurate evaluation of a trim requires knowing how balance looks, both at the level of the hoof itself and higher up the leg. These skills must be learned and take practice to develop. The time and effort involved, however, are a good investment, because the knowledge helps owners understand and meet the trimming needs of their animals. An added benefit is that the ability to evaluate balance correctly and recognize hoof condition is an essential part of appraising conformation, which is a great help to anyone who buys or breeds horses.

# 6

## Sizing up a Shoeing Job

Farriers must apply a broad base of knowledge and skill to choose the right shoes and apply them correctly. These abilities, combined with skill at trimming, creativity, and professional ethics, are what separate the true professionals from the rest.

There are people who claim to be professional horseshoers but who show up without the tools—or the intention—to change the shape of shoes from the way that they come out of the box. Some will even claim that the manufacturers have scientifically designed a perfectly shaped horseshoe and that the horse's feet should be modified to fit the shoes. The next step up from this backwards approach is the bumper banger, who uses the truck bumper as an anvil and bangs the shoe a few times to spread it out or close it a little. Usually this will make it possible to drive the nails into the hoof wall where they belong. These shoers carry two sizes of shoes, small and smaller, and one size of nails, big.

At the other end of the spectrum is the shoer who hauls a trailer that is a mobile machine shop. In addition to a forge and anvil, there may be a drill press, arc and gas welders, a band saw, assorted hand power tools, a pad cutter, and a grinding wheel. This person carries six or seven sizes of shoes in five styles, as well as a dozen sizes of straight bar steel. Mounted floodlights provide the finishing touch to disperse shadows while the shoer videotapes the horse at various gaits.

It does not require a machine shop to shoe a horse properly. Tools do not make a good shoer; using them creatively does. I admit that having a large array of power tools will sometimes save time. As in any trade or profession, however, there are key tools that are necessary to do the job properly. I would be very skeptical of anyone attempting to shoe a horse with less than the tools shown in figure 6.1, which can handle most basic shoeing jobs. By basic, I mean work done on animals with healthy feet and good hoof walls, requiring no major corrective measures, and that have a hoof shape that lends itself to the use of stock shoes (see chap. 8). Unfortunately, many horses do not fit this description.

Some important shoe modifications that are necessary to deal with certain problems

**Figure 6.1** Basic tools necessary to shoe a horse (from the bottom up): hoof rasp, hoof gauge, clincher, pull-offs, nippers, driving hammer, clinch block, hoof knife (resting on base of anvil), anvil, shaping hammer, and shoeing apron.

**Figure 6.2** Basic forging tools: (A) forge for heating steel; (B) anvil; (C) anvil devil, a sharp hardened steel triangle for cutting steel bar stock; (D) one-and-a-half-pound hammer; (E) fire tongs for holding hot metal; (F) punches for making nail holes; (G) cross-peen hammer; (H) ball-peen hammer; (I) two-pound hammer; (J) creaser (this tool is struck with a hammer to form a groove for nails); (K) spring-operated vise; (L) quench bucket; (M) wire brush; (N) small sledgehammer.

can be accomplished only if the steel is heated to make it malleable (soft and bendable). Clips, calks, trailers, square toes, and rocker toes are examples of these shoe modifications (chap. 8). If a forge for heating the steel and a few additional blacksmithing items such as fire tongs, metal punches, and assorted hammers are available, almost any shoeing job can be handled (fig. 6.2). Other tools and equipment (for instance, a grinding wheel) are useful for saving time rather than pure necessities. Each farrier will choose which timesaving tools are best suited, based on the types of horses seen and the space limitations of the vehicle.

With this information, the owner should be able to tell at a glance if a prospective horseshoer has adequate equipment to do the job right. The next step, recognizing how well the tools are used, is more difficult. It would simplify matters if we could measure the worker's skill by how tools are held or swung. Unfortunately, we can only judge the results. Several factors should be looked for when examining a shoeing job for quality: fit, nailing, and finish work. Whether the overall job achieves the desired effects should also be considered.

## PROPER FIT

A properly fitted horseshoe will be flush with the edge of the hoof wall except in the heel area and a small portion of the part of the wall called the quarters (fig. 6.3). Behind the nail closest to the heel, starting where the hoof wall curves inward and continuing beyond the heel itself, a small amount of shoe should be exposed (fig. 6.4). This expansion area serves three purposes: it allows room for the naturally occurring

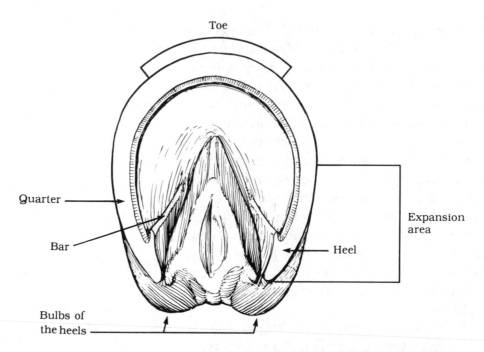

Toe

Quarter

Bar

Heel

Expansion area

Bulbs of the heels

**Figure 6.3**  The parts of the hoof wall.

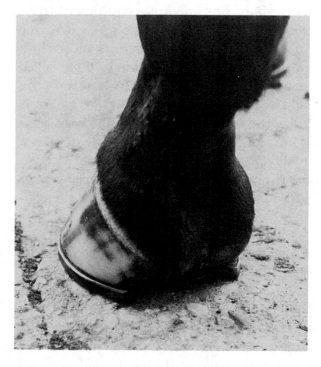

**Figure 6.4**  This foot is shod with good expansion room, starting where the hoof curves inward toward the heel and continuing beyond the heel. This practice provides room for the hoof to expand and contract.

expansion and contraction of the horse's hooves, it helps prevent the hoof wall from running over the edge of the shoe as the foot grows longer, and it gives the horse a solid base of support.

To give a horse a wide, supportive foundation and not interfere with the hoof's natural concussion-absorbing qualities, a shoe should be fitted as fully as possible. How much expansion room to allow will vary somewhat depending on the circumstances, but a rule of thumb would be approximately the thickness of a dime. More can be an advantage, and less would be prudent for a horse that lives in a muddy pasture (where the suction of the mud works at the nails) or tends to step on its own feet a lot. Some activities that involve extremely tight turns, such as barrel racing, do not permit leaving as much expansion room. Stepping on the edge of another foot's shoe in a tight turn can pull a shoe or, worse, cause a fall. A horse shod without much expansion room may require more frequent resets to prevent the hoof wall from running over the edge of the shoe.

The heels of the shoe extend well beyond the hoof heels to ease stress at the fetlock joint by shifting the weight rearward under the bony column and to protect the bulbs of the heels. These benefits may have to be compromised with shorter heels if a horse overreaches (bumps the heels of the front feet with the toes of the hind feet) or is a chronic fence pawer. The horse's heels should always be completely covered by the shoe, and unless there is a good reason to do otherwise, a minimum of 1/4 inch of shoe on the front feet and 3/8 inch on the hind feet should extend behind the hoof. When needed, extra support can be offered by extending the shoe heels even farther back beyond the hoof.

The last important aspect of shoe fit is the levelness of the shoe. If the hoof is missing chunks or has broken-down quarters, sometimes the rest of the hoof wall cannot be trimmed short enough to be even (fig. 6.5). In this case there is no way to avoid gaps between shoe and hoof. If the shoe can be nailed securely, it should cause no problems. If these gaps are very large, the risk of a cast shoe can be greatly reduced by filling the empty spaces with one of the strong but flexible hoof repair/filler compounds that are available. The only time there should be a gap between the hoof heel and the shoe, however, is when corrective measures are being taken for a serious quarter crack (usually in conjunction with a bar shoe) or as treatment for a condition called sheared heels, where the heels of the foot are uneven

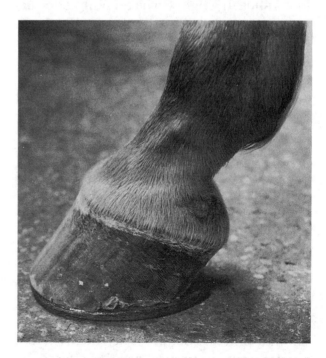

**Figure 6.5** Even though there is a gap between shoe and hoof through the quarters, the toe and heel have good contact and the shoe is securely nailed.

from the bulbs down. These two problems are discussed further in chapter 7.

The description of proper shoe fit, allowing for minor adjustments in expansion room and heel length, will hold true in most cases. There are numerous corrective measures, however, that will deviate from this model. Chapter 8 describes and discusses some common examples of specialized shoes. There is little need for an owner to worry about not being able to tell the difference between poor shoe fit and corrective shoeing. Anytime a shoer takes corrective action, it is done with forethought to accomplish a specific goal. Ask for an explanation of the reasons if it is not offered. Most good shoers, like other craftsmen, take pride in their work. If they see that the owner is interested, they will be happy to explain what they are doing to help the horse move better or have healthier feet.

## NAILING

Nailing is not the mysterious process some people imagine. It is true that room for error is very small, but the nails are designed for their special job. Unlike other nails, they are made so they will bend when driven. To allow bending, each nail has a relatively thin, flat shank and a bevel on one side of the tip (fig. 6.6). When the nail is driven into the hoof wall, it bends away from the resistance placed on the bevel as it is pushed through the horn material (fig. 6.7). A harder hammer blow creates greater resistance, causing the nail to bend more and emerge at a lower point in the hoof wall. Light tapping allows the nail to travel fairly straight. A mark on one side of the head makes it easy to know in which direction the nail will bend. There are many tricks to good nailing, but proper initial placement and management of the arc are the primary means of controlling nail height. Furthermore, placement of the nail holes in the shoe—or, when a machine-manufactured shoe is used, selection of the proper holes—all affect the quality of the results.

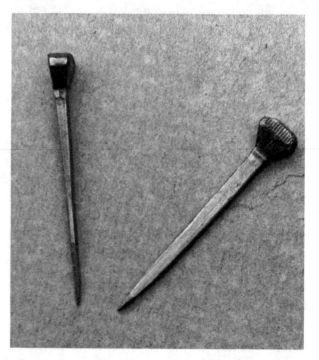

**Figure 6.6** Standard shoeing nail (enlarged). Note the flat shank and the beveled tip.

**Figure 6.7** Two ways to drive a shoeing nail: (A) A nail tapped lightly will travel fairly straight. (B) Striking harder will create resistance against the bevel and make the nail bend away from sensitive structures.

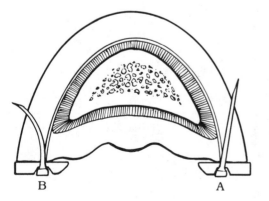

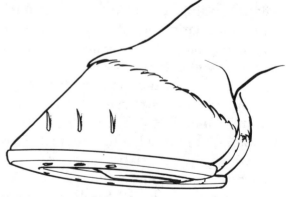

As a general rule, nails should not be placed in the expansion area. This incorrect but fairly common practice defeats the purpose of leaving room on the shoe to accommodate the natural expansion and contraction of the hoof. It will reduce the hoof's shock-absorbing qualities and can, over time, lead to a condition called contracted heels as well as to concussion-related lameness. Shoers who use machine-manufactured shoes exclusively are often faced with this dilemma, because the back nail hole in the common brands often falls in the expansion area. Chapter 8 takes a closer look at this problem.

Proper nail height will vary from horse to horse and sometimes from foot to foot. The basic premise is to drive the nails up high enough to get a good hold on healthy, sound hoof wall. On average, this is 5/8 inch to 1 inch above the bottom edge of the hoof. A very low nail (less than 3/8 inch up) will often pull through the hoof wall before the next shoeing is due, leaving a stumpy clinched nail hanging. Generally these short, bent-over nails pose no threat, but they also do not help secure the shoe. A very high nail, on the other hand, poses the slightly increased risk that an undetected kink will irritate the sensitive living tissue. Regardless of how high the nail is, if the shank does not come close to living tissue, this problem will not occur. There are other reasons, however, to avoid nails so high that less than 1/4 inch emerges from the hoof wall. Toward the point of a nail, the shank gradually tapers to a very thin tip, so a clinch made from a very high nail will be small. Because nail clinches tend to rust on exposure, the thin metal of tiny, high clinches

## NAIL PLACEMENT

sometimes rusts through, releasing their grip on the hoof wall. Additionally, the hole left behind can interfere with nailing the next time the horse is shod.

In an ideal situation, when a shoe is pulled for a reset, there will be two rows of nail holes on each side of the hoof, one row from the shoe just pulled and, below it, one row from the previous shoeing or reset. The oldest row will be cut off during trimming, leaving the other nearer the ground. A shoe is then nailed in place, creating a new row above the remaining one (fig. 6.8). Constant hoof growth makes this cycle possible, and the integrity of the hoof wall is not compromised by too many nail holes.

The cyclical placement of nails works this neatly only if there are no obstacles. There is no sense in creating a nice straight row of nails if one or more lands in a cracked

**Figure 6.8** The oldest nail holes have been trimmed off. This is a neat new row of nail stubs (before finish work) above the row of holes remaining from the last shoeing.

portion of the hoof wall. Not only will those nails offer little shoe support, they are likely to spread the crack even more. Weak spots, missing chunks, and holes from old nails driven out of line to avoid past problems will often force a deviation from the ideal.

One more variable is worth mentioning: the horse. If we visualize the task of driving a nail, then imagine that the object we are nailing is wiggling around or sometimes, with little warning, leaning hundreds of pounds on us or pulling with equal force, it is easy to understand compromises on a perfectly placed straight line of nails. Fortunately, these compromises need not detract from the main goal of nailing: to avoid sensitive tissue and secure the shoe to sound hoof.

## NUMBER OF NAILS

A common misconception is that because there are eight nail holes in most factory-made shoes, a shoe is not properly attached unless all the holes are filled. Particularly in the smaller shoe sizes, the standard eight nail holes are there to give the shoer a choice. A shoer should use six, seven, or eight nails to secure each shoe. It makes good sense to put as few holes in a hoof as are necessary to hold the shoe on. This will depend on the type of shoe used, the size of the foot, the condition of the hoof wall, and whether the horse is in general difficult to keep shoes on. A small foot, comparable to a 00 (double aught) or 0 (aught) size requires only six nails (fig. 6.9 and 6.10). Six nails will sometimes be adequate for a size 1 foot (fig. 6.11), although seven or eight are generally in order. Anything larger will generally require at least seven and usually eight nails.

**Figure 6.9** Size 00 (double aught) machine-manufactured shoe (actual size).

**Figure 6.10** Size 0 (aught) machine-manufactured shoe (actual size).

**Figure 6.11** Size 1 machine-manufactured shoe (actual size).

When a nail penetrates the sensitive living tissue inside the hoof, it is called pricking the horse. Although uncommon, this can be done even by a skilled professional. It is most likely to happen to horses with thin hoof walls, and the potential is greater for animals that refuse to stand still. Some horses will jump sky-high when pricked, whereas for others the only way to tell is when a drop of blood is seen on the tip of the nail. For this reason, nail tips should be checked whenever there is any possibility of a problem.

If properly treated, a pricked horse should have no long-term problems. The nail is pulled out, a penetrating antiseptic like turpentine is poured into the hole, and a new nail is driven through a different part of the hoof. The professional will then inquire whether the horse's tetanus vaccination is current. If not, a booster shot is recommended.

A more serious problem is a nail that does not penetrate living tissue but is close enough to cause irritation. In these uncommon cases the nail causes the area to become inflamed, and ultimately some cells die. An abscess forms inside the hoof, and the horse becomes lame, generally about three days after being shod. Pulling the shoe will help relieve the pressure, and the hoof should be soaked in a strong Epsom salts solution to encourage the abscess to drain. Seeking a veterinarian's advice about using antibiotics to combat infection is prudent. If an abscess in a hoof is not open, it will normally work its way up the inside of the hoof wall and burst at the coronary band. The horse will remain lame until the internal pressure is relieved.

## NAILING MISHAPS

**FINISH WORK**  When trimming is complete and the shoe has been nailed on, small nail stubs will be sticking out both sides of the hoof (fig. 6.8). At this stage, everything done to complete the shoeing is called finish work. The nail stubs are turned into small, flat squares that are folded down and embedded in depressions that are either filed or notched into the hoof wall (fig. 6.12). Because these metal squares (clinches) are largely responsible for holding a shoe on, they must be sturdy. They should not be too strong, however. A powerful animal like a horse is able to pull off a shoe if, for instance, the shoe gets hooked on a fence or is held down by another foot. If the clinches do not give by either straightening or breaking, the nails will tear through the hoof wall. This can make shoe replacement very difficult. For this reason, after the clinches are turned down they should be filed flush with the hoof. If they are properly seated in the depressions, there will be plenty of strength to secure the shoe under normal conditions but not so much that they won't give if necessary. Another reason for filing clinches is to smooth them so we don't get cut when picking up a horse's feet (fig. 6.13).

If a foot is properly trimmed and prepared and the shoe is well fitted, there should be little need for rasping the hoof itself once the shoe is in place. Sometimes, when a shoe is nailed on, the hoof wall will expand by as much as the thickness of a nail. It may protrude over the edge of the shoe and can be rasped away without harm.

An improper method some shoers employ is called "dubbing the toe"—rasping away as much as 1/2 inch or more of hoof wall that hangs over the front of the shoe (fig. 6.14). In these cases the shoe is too

**(b)**

**(a)**

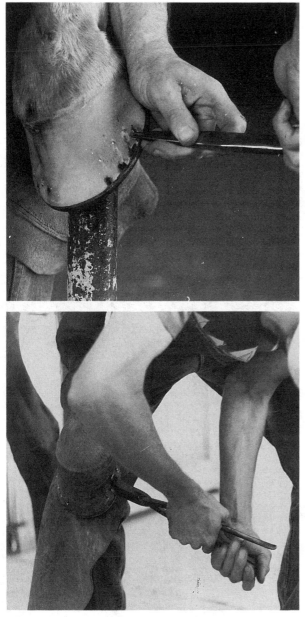

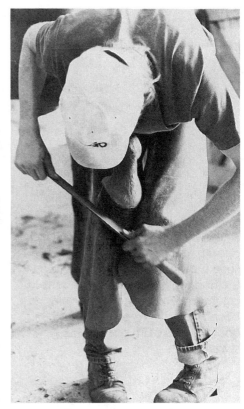

**Figure 6.12** (a) Filing a groove under the nail stubs to seat the clinches in; (b) notching individual depressions for each nail; (c) using the clinchers to bend the nail stub, forming the clinch, and seating it in the depression.

**(c)**

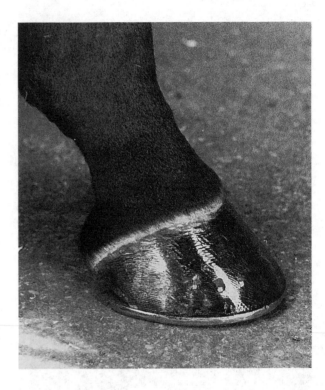

**Figure 6.13** Small, neat clinches, filed smooth to allow them to break if the shoe is pulled off instead of damaging the hoof wall. This practice also avoids cut fingers. The new and old holes have been filled with wood putty, and the hoof wall has been coated with a sealant.

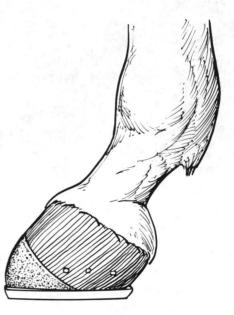

**Figure 6.14** The toe has been dubbed to meet the shoe so as to give the appearance of a proper fit.

small, or poor nailing technique causes it to slide back. This rasping will weaken the hoof wall, decrease the weight-bearing surface, and change the flight pattern of the leg. Dubbing the toe should not be confused with shoeing a horse with square-toe shoes, which also involves rasping hoof wall at the toe (see chap. 8).

Some shoers find it useful to fill both new and old nail holes with wood putty. Combined with the use of a quality hoof sealant, this practice helps maintain the hoof moisture balance, restoring the natural moisture barrier, which the nail holes have disrupted, to what we started with or better. The extra cost of the sealant and the time it takes to apply it may warrant an additional charge, which is nevertheless a worthwhile investment.

Many variables must be considered when judging a shoeing job. It is important to remember, though, that a shoeing job is only as good as the trim it rests on. The best pair of handmade shoes, perfectly shaped and perfectly nailed, will not avoid the problems caused by poor trimming. Too many fancy corrective shoeing jobs are merely attempts to solve problems that spring from incorrect trimming. Many gait flaws and minor hoof deformities can be resolved, and unbalanced horses helped, with nothing more than plain flat shoes and a balanced trim.

The horse owner can learn to recognize a properly balanced trim, understand the basic mechanics of a shoeing job, and realistically appraise a horse's natural conformation problems. Such owners are prepared to judge a shoer's work fairly, protect themselves and their horses against incompetence, and discuss important shoeing-related decisions.

In fairness, owners should wait until the shoer is finished with a job before judging the results. Looking over the shoer's shoulder presents a safety hazard, not to mention that it will not encourage the best work. Most confident professionals appreciate an informed and interested customer, but owners who involve themselves in every cut of the nippers and every blow of the hammer only waste the shoer's valuable time. A quality shoer is likely to replace these owners with someone else. It is permissible to interrupt a shoer to ask for an explanation, but keep in mind that most shoeing-related problems develop over time. It is therefore better to do a thorough evaluation of the finished job. If necessary, seek an explanation at that time, and if you are not satisfied, try someone else.

Remember also that it is not possible for anyone to do every part of every job perfectly. With a good understanding of the process, however, you can judge whether, overall, the work quality meets your horse's needs. Once this is determined, you can relax and confidently place your trust in the competent professional you have found to take care of your horse's hooves.

# 7

# Lameness and Other Problems

Human interference has subdued natural selection in the domestic horse. By giving horses shelter, flakes of hay, and buckets of high-protein grain, as well as providing veterinary and farrier services, over the centuries we intervened in this natural process. Additionally, and perhaps more important, we have gradually taken over nature's role of selecting horses for breeding, and we do not always choose the best traits. Too many breeders pay more attention to characteristics like color than to conformation and soundness. Because of this the course of natural selection has been distorted, problems are bound to emerge.

In the wild, natural processes weed out the weakest horses from a herd. The first to go are the animals that cannot keep up with the group's movement because of lameness. In this way the gene pool is purged of horses that are predisposed to leg and hoof problems. Furthermore, because of their relationship with us, horses perform functions very different from those they were designed for. For instance, in nature a herd of horses wanders much of the day while grazing and needs only occasional short bursts of speed to avoid danger. Constant walking over varied terrain not only keeps the hooves naturally trimmed, it also encourages good circulation in the legs and feet. Most domestic horses are confined to relatively small spaces. They no longer move around to get enough to eat; rather, they stand still much of the time and then, at our convenience, get a lot of exercise all at once.

The combination of these genetic and environmental factors makes horses prone to myriad problems. One problem arising from environmental influences is thrush infection, which I will discuss later. There are numerous genetically caused problems that would be self-regulating in nature. A good example is a horse with extremely poor leg conformation in the form of misaligned joints. The animal is likely to suffer chronic lameness, such as strained tendons, or its joints may become arthritic. Eventually, out of necessity, the animal is taken out of service but all too often is foolishly allocated to the back lot as a broodmare. This practice simply allows the undesirable traits to survive into another generation. In nature, this horse would be left behind by the herd and therefore re-moved from the gene pool.

Since a result of our influence on the equine world is that horses are more sus-ceptible to some types of problems, we now have the ongoing obligation to care for these creatures so as to avoid these maladies. Unfortunately, even with the best of care, trouble will sometimes arise. Following is a discussion of some of the more common hoof and leg conditions and kinds of lame-ness facing horse owners.

## HOOF DRYNESS

In a healthy, moist, and flexible foot, the frog and the heel bulbs will give to moderate finger pressure, and even the sole will compress slightly. A dry hoof will feel ex-tremely hard, including the sole, frog, and heel bulbs (page 28, fig. 2.15). This is im-portant because hooves that are too dry, having lost their flexibility, are less able to absorb concussion and are prone to crack. It takes practice to differentiate a normal hoof from an overly dry hoof.

Hoof dryness can be caused by lack of enough fresh drinking water, evaporation owing to very dry weather, or poor circula-tion caused by insufficient exercise. Good circulation is the key, since this internal mechanism works to maintain optimum moisture balance.

The first line of defense against dry feet is making sure the animal always has access to plenty of fresh water and is given regular moderate exercise. Assuming that a horse has sufficient internal moisture, the next step is to keep the moisture inside rather than letting it evaporate into the atmos-phere.

Sealing the hoof wall with a good commercial hoof sealant will dramatically reduce evaporation (fig. 7.1). This practice is particularly useful when the outer layer of the hoof wall, which is designed to reduce evaporation, has been disturbed by the rasping and nailing of the shoeing operation. Sealing the hoof wall, combined with providing free access to drinking water and regular exercise, is the best way to control hoof moisture balance.

The flexibility of the hoof can be increased, if necessary, by introducing moisture from the outside. A horse can be stood in a creek, the edge of a pond, or a man-made puddle. There is some controversy among farriers on whether this offers a long-term solution, because a dry hoof is missing more than plain water. This soaking does at least temporarily make the feet

**Figure 7.1** The shiny coating is a hoof sealant. A quality product will last for an entire shoeing cycle.

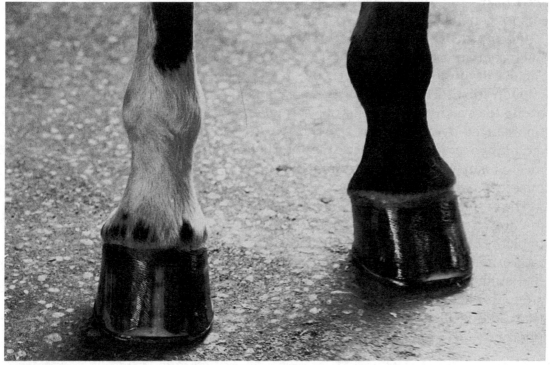

flexible, restoring comfort and normal hoof function so exercise can be undertaken. Exercise in turn stimulates circulation, which does offer a long-term solution. It should be noted though that the problem of hoof dryness can be made worse if a horse is regularly allowed to stand in drying mud. As the mud drys it draws moisture out of the hoof rather than adds to it.

In my opinion most of the greasy hoof preparations are not sufficient treatment. They do not penetrate far enough or provide the complex combination of electrolytes found in hoof moisture. Their value, if any, may be in slowing evaporation. Some of the less greasy products seem to penetrate better, and some have nutritive value. These may be of some benefit when applied to the coronary band, sole, frog, and heel bulbs.

There isn't much a shoer can do about the condition other than to use a sealant and make recommendations, but dry hooves do present some problems in shoeing. In a hot, dry summer, hooves can become so dry and hard that they are very difficult to cut with nippers, and it can be nearly impossible to trim the sole and frog with a hoof knife. To make shoeing easier, an owner can soak a horse's hard, dry feet for thirty minutes, allowing time for the surface to dry before the shoer arrives.

## POOR HOOF QUALITY

Animals with weak hooves present a special shoeing problem. Generally their hoof walls don't hold up well without shoes, but it can be difficult to securely fasten a shoe to a soft, flaky, weak, or crumbly hoof (fig. 7.2). Clips are frequently necessary to add support and take some of the burden off the nails. Clips are discussed in chapter 8.

**Figure 7.2** A weak hoof wall has made the shoe easy to cast, taking a lot of the wall with it. In such cases, shoes are hard to secure adequately.

Apart from hereditary influences, the common reasons for poor hoof quality are nutritional deficiencies, disease, and excessive hoof moisture. Additionally, older horses commonly have poor hoof quality and slow hoof growth. Whatever the cause, proper nutrition and regular exercise to stimulate circulation are a must. Excessive moisture, which tends to soften the hoof, can result from soggy pastures or sometimes from overzealous owners trying to resolve a dryness problem. The solution begins when the cause is removed.

When soft hoof walls are a problem, it is often beneficial for the shoer to sear the bottom of the hoof wall with a hot shoe (fig. 7.3). This melts the horn tubules shut, which will stop moisture from being wicked up from the ground, as well as decreasing loss of internal moisture by evaporation. As a regular shoeing practice, hot-fitting shoes in this way is harmless and sometimes very beneficial.

In some instances, where nutrition is the issue, dietary supplements, particularly biotin, a component of the vitamin B complex, and the mineral selenium (especially in regions where the soil is deficient in selenium, so it is not present in the local hay and grain), can make a big difference. A veterinarian should be consulted for product and dose recommendations.

Note, however, that any change of hoof quality due to improved nutrition takes place in the new growth, not in the existing hoof material. This means that it takes a minimum of four to five months of supplements before the change is noticeable. Improvement becomes apparent then because at this point nearly half of the hoof wall is new growth that has benefited from

**Figure 7.3** Smoke drifts off the bottom of the hoof wall as the hot (not red-hot) shoe melts the horn tubules shut, reducing evaporation. This painless process takes less time than cooling a shoe each time the fit is checked.

the enhanced nutrition. In most cases the dietary regimen must be continued indefinitely to maintain healthier hooves.

Some horses have thin, weak hoof walls because of their genetic makeup. Proper nutrition, good stable management, and regular hoof care will make the best of difficult circumstances. This trait should certainly be considered when deciding whether to breed an animal.

## HOOF CRACKS

When discussing hoof cracks, it is important to differentiate between hairline, superficial cracks and more serious cracks that extend through the wall. Thin surface cracks may be a sign of other problems like hoof dryness, but they don't themselves cause any real difficulties.

A hoof wall that is split all the way through to the laminae, from ground level up to or near the coronary band, however, can cause serious problems, including lameness. Difficulties arise in two ways. First, a crack opens a pathway for infection by allowing bacteria to get directly to the sensitive structures of the hoof. Second, a crack through the wall will spread open with weight bearing and squeeze shut when weight is lifted. This movement can cause the internal tissues to alternately be torn and pinched, a painful condition that will cause lameness. A small amount of blood or serum can be seen near the top of the crack.

Dryness or poor-quality hoof material can contribute significantly to hoof cracking but is not generally the cause. Hooves crack when pressure on the hoof exceeds the hoof wall's ability to withstand stress. In these cases the problem can be traced to hoof-pounding activities, often combined with a hoof imbalance that causes distorted hoof growth and places extra weight-bearing strain on one portion of the foot. Often these cracks start at the bottom and, unless stopped, work their way up to the coronary band (fig. 7.4). As new, intact hoof grows down from the coronary band, the outward pressure of the two sides of the crack causes the new growth to split. If the hoof wall on both sides of the crack can be stabilized, the leverage will no longer have this effect, and the hoof wall will grow down intact.

Long before a crack reaches the coronary band, a horseshoer will try to stop its upward movement. Balanced trimming is an obvi-

**Figure 7.4** In most cases a toe crack starts at ground level and spreads upward.

ous first step. Immediately above the crack, a groove is filed in the hoof wall, or a crescent-shaped slot is melted in with a hot iron (fig. 7.5). This measure is intended to spread the stress of the crack horizontally across the hoof and in some cases will stop the upward progress of the split. Additionally, the groove will act as a marker to map the crack's development.

There are many approaches a shoer may try when confronted with an advancing hoof crack. Clips are commonly used to keep the hoof wall immobilized on the rigid shoe surface (chap. 8). In some cases it may be necessary to wire or otherwise lace the hoof wall on one side of the crack to the other side. To successfully lace a crack may require cutting a deep groove along the crack's length, which ensures the removal of any infection. At this point a hoof repair bonding compound may be used to seal, protect, and add stability to the area. Whatever the approach, when the two sides are held together, the new hoof growth is not pulled apart and grows down intact.

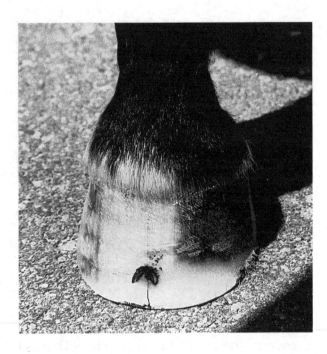

**Figure 7.5** A crescent-shaped slot has been melted into the hoof wall with a hot iron. This often stops the crack's progress. The hoof has also had a balanced trim and been sculpted to achieve symmetry, which distributes weight bearing more evenly.

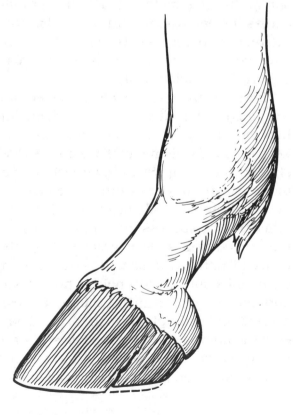

**Figure 7.6** One approach is to trim back the heel side of a quarter crack so it bears no weight. The leverage to spread the crack is removed. A bar shoe is then applied to distribute weight evenly around the rest of the hoof and provide an adequate bearing surface. Adding frog pressure with a pad or with the bar of the shoe is often useful in these cases.

A crack within a few inches of the hoof heel is called a quarter crack. One treatment approach for a crack here is to trim the hoof wall on the heel side of the crack short enough so it bears no weight (fig. 7.6). This takes the pressure off the crack, again allowing new hoof to grow intact. A bar shoe with a pad to maintain frog pressure would normally be used to distribute weight bearing evenly around the rest of the hoof (chap. 8).

Small horizontal cracks can form at the coronary band when the normal production of hoof horn material is disrupted. A minor injury to that portion of the coronary band from a rock or another foot can be the cause, as can a minor infection in the white line that works its way up the inside of the hoof wall, breaking out at the coronary band. It has been reported that a tiny pebble jammed into the white line can occasionally take the same course. These small cracks do not usually cause any major problems. As they grow down closer to ground level, clips may be used to keep a small crack from getting larger.

The cracks most difficult to deal with are those caused by wire cuts or other serious injury to the coronary band. These injuries can cause a permanent weakness or crack in the hoof below the damaged point. Creative ongoing treatment may be needed to keep the horse sound.

## THRUSH

Thrush is an anaerobic (lives without oxygen) fungus infection that attacks the frog of a horse's foot. It is common in stalled horses, particularly if the stall is not kept clean, which includes replacing the bedding with fresh, dry material daily. Nowhere in nature would a horse stand around in its own manure with urine-soaked organic material packed in the crevices around the frog, creating the perfect environment for thrush.

Thrush can be identified by its black, mushy appearance, but mostly by the objectionable smell unleashed during hoof picking. Not only does it smell bad, but the odor will linger tenaciously on hands and clothing that have touched the infected area. Just ask my wife!

Thrush does not generally cause lameness unless it is allowed to destroy a large portion of the frog. A serious thrush infection, likely to cause lameness usually involves the central cleft of the frog rather than the commissures between frog and sole. In these cases, which are difficult to treat, some concussion-absorbing and circulatory function, normally provided by the frog, is lost. Furthermore, if the disease progresses far enough, sensitive tissue can become affected or left unprotected by the diminished frog (fig. 7.7).

Resolving a thrush infection requires a cooperative effort between shoer or veterinarian and owner. As much of the infected tissue as possible should be trimmed away by the vet or shoer. This exposes most of the remaining fungus to oxygen and also makes it accessible for further treatment by the owner.

The owner's job is twofold, each part of equal importance. First, the living environment must be kept clean and dry. Second, the hoof should be cleaned out regularly (to expose the tissue to oxygen again), and an antifungal solution should be poured on and around the frog (fig. 7.8). A special point should be made of prying open all the

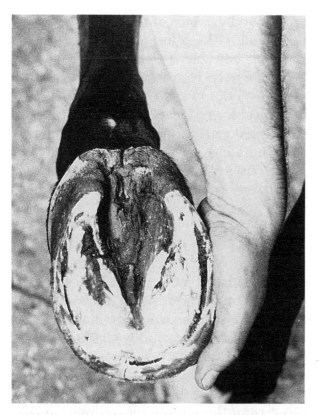

**Figure 7.7** The frog has been severely diminished by a thrush infection. The lack of weight-bearing pressure on the frog has allowed the heels to become contracted (too close together). Contracted heels reduce shock absorption.

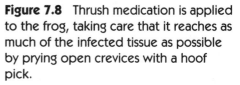

**Figure 7.8** Thrush medication is applied to the frog, taking care that it reaches as much of the infected tissue as possible by prying open crevices with a hoof pick.

cracks and crevices of the frog with a hoof pick to allow the solution to reach as much tissue as possible. There are several excellent commercial antifungal preparations: all will do the job. If used diligently, a 10 percent chlorine bleach solution will also be effective. If you start with a freshly trimmed frog and a clean environment, ten days of conscientious hoof picking and antithrush medication will resolve most thrush infections.

## GREASED HEELS

Greased heels (also called scratches) is a form of dermatitis that affects the soft skin on the back of the pastern above the heel bulbs. It usually starts with chapped skin caused by damp or muddy conditions, but any skin irritation at this site can develop into greased heels. The affected area develops a mass of scabs, which can crack and bleed from the stretching common to this area. There may be a greasy discharge. To maintain skin flexibility and encourage healing, the area must be kept clean, and a medicated salve should be applied.

## SOLE BRUISES AND ABSCESSES

Minor damage caused by compression of any area of the sensitive sole is called a sole bruise. As in any bruise, tiny capillaries are disturbed, and the spot becomes tender.

There are two common causes for sole bruising. One cause is associated mostly with being unshod, and the other results when a horseshoe puts pressure directly on the sole. Walking or running across rocky terrain or coarse gravel is often enough to cause bruising, particularly in an unshod horse. When the point of a rock compresses the sole, internal tissue is damaged. The injured capillaries release a small amount of blood, which accumulates inside. This gives the bruise its characteristic reddish purple appearance, often seen when the sole is trimmed during shoeing.

If the hoof grows over the edge of a shoe heel or the shoe was fitted too narrow at the heels to begin with, weight-bearing pressure is placed on the sole in the V between the bar and the outside edge of the hoof wall (fig. 7.9). This bruises the tissue in the same way a rock would, except that the pressure continues each time a step is taken. If the cause is not removed, the constant irritation can cause the bruise to develop into a corn (a deep bruise that is difficult to treat). If the tissue is damaged badly enough to kill a large group of cells, an abscess—a painful pus pocket—may form at the site.

Sole bruises can range from a little uncomfortable to very painful for the horse. A horseshoer will often trim the bruised area to make it less likely to bear weight and to be certain no abscess is present. Applying shoes to an unshod horse is frequently all that is needed to help it move comfortably again. When the bruise is caused by the shoe itself, the sole is trimmed back to take pressure off it, and the shoe is fitted fuller so the hoof wall rests completely on the steel, with no direct pressure to the sole.

If an abscess exists, it must be opened to allow drainage. The shoer can often accomplish this by paring away only as much dead sole as would normally be removed during trimming. The owner should then clean the hoof, apply peroxide, and soak the foot at least twice daily in a strong Epsom salts solution. Cotton can be used between soakings to fill the hole and keep dirt from getting packed in, or an old sock

**Figure 7.9**  Direct shoe pressure on the sole can cause bruising.

**Figure 7.10** A small sole puncture healed over and formed an abscess, which followed the course of least resistance and undermined the sole. The abscess has been opened to allow it to drain and keep it from healing over and again trapping the infection inside. The foot must be soaked, medicated, and kept clean and dry.

can be pulled over the hoof and taped in place to keep the dirt out. In general, however, a veterinarian is the first person to call and is the best resource for developing a treatment plan if a horse is lame and an abscess is suspected.

Whether the abscess was caused by a bad bruise, a puncture wound, or a misdirected shoeing nail, it must remain open and be soaked regularly until the wound is completely healed. If the outer part of the wound heals first, enclosing the infection, the abscess will spread, taking the course of least resistance. This means it will work its way up the inside of the wall and burst at the coronary band or spread between the sensitive and insensitive soles, finally coming out when the pressure is great enough (fig. 7.10). The horse will usually be lame until the pressure is relieved.

**SHEARED HEELS** The condition called sheared heels exists when the two heel bulbs on a foot are not at the same height above the ground and the coronary band is correspondingly distorted (fig. 7.11). The internal structures slide across each other, or shear, as one side moves upward and the other remains stationary—hence the name sheared heels. When the shearing exceeds the flexibility of the tissue, internal damage causes the horse to become sore and eventually lame.

Sheared heels develops over time because of uneven weight distribution, which can be caused by faulty conformation or by consistently unbalanced trimming. The side of the heel that bears excessive weight is forced upward, and the shape of the foot is distorted. To bring the heels back into alignment, the high side must sink down to its original position. Achieving this begins with a balanced trim. Before the shoe is nailed on, the hoof heel on the high side has an additional wedge trimmed off so that when the shoe is secured a gap will exist and this heel will not rest on the shoe (fig. 7.12). The heel thus has room to sink, pulling the bulb and coronary band down. Often the heel will move enough to meet the

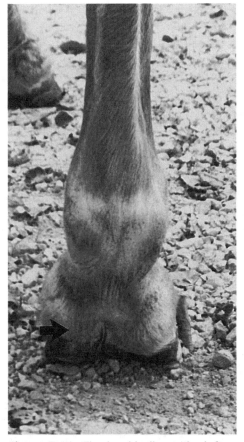

**Figure 7.11** The heel bulb on the left side (arrow) has been pushed upward, out of alignment with the right heel bulb. This case of sheared heels caused the horse enough discomfort that it limped.

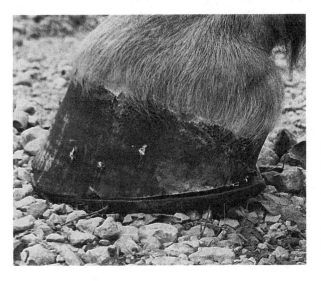

**Figure 7.12** Leaving a gap on the side of the high heel bulb allows it to sink down to the shoe, which often happens within a few minutes. This trimming should be done a little at a time, so the extent of the shear will determine how many shoeings it will take to bring the heels into alignment.

shoe within minutes. The amount of shear will dictate the number of shoeings necessary to get the two heels aligned. Once alignment is achieved, care must be taken to maintain balance and avoid stressing the attachment between the heels. This offers the best opportunity for healing and for the return of strength to the tissue.

**SPLINTS** The splint bones are the two long, narrow, triangular bones behind the cannon bone (fig. 7.13). Their job is to provide additional support for the bones of the knee in the front leg and the hock in the hind leg. In addition, the space between the splint bones provides a large, protected depression for the passage of blood vessels, nerves, tendons, and ligaments.

Until a horse is about six years old, the splint bones are attached to the cannon bone by ligaments. During this time, if excessive pressure is placed on the splint bones by overwork, uneven weight bearing, or injury, the attachment between splint bone and cannon bone is torn. The horse's body will deposit an abnormal amount of calcium (a process called exostosis) in order to repair the damage. Calcium therefore is not introduced evenly to fuse the bones as would normally happen as the horse matures, but is deposited in lumps at the damaged places (fig. 7.14). This condition is known as a splint.

This problem is most common on the medial (closest to the midline of the animal) splint bones of the front legs. This inside splint bone articulates with two bones of the knee instead of one, as does the lateral (farthest from the midline) splint, therefore supporting extra weight. A young horse

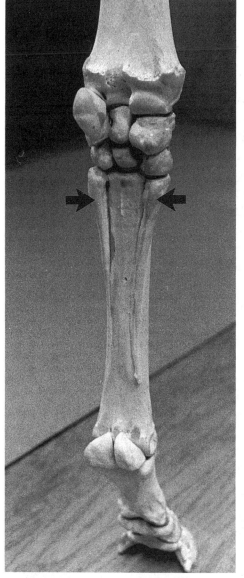

**Figure 7.13** Each leg has two splint bones (arrows).

**Figure 7.14** This X ray shows the development of a calcium lump (arrow) resulting from damage to the attachment between the splint bone and cannon bone. The lump can be felt through the skin.

that is worked harder than its bone and muscle development can handle is a prime candidate for splints. A dietary excess of the mineral phosphorus has also been tied to this condition.

The damage and irritation at the site are painful and will cause temporary lameness. Once the calcification is complete the irritation will cease, and in most cases the lumps become only cosmetic blemishes. Long-term problems occasionally occur when the location of the permanent hard lump causes it to interfere with tendons and ligaments.

The best approach to dealing with splints is to avoid the problem by a gradual conditioning program, balanced nutrition, and protective boots or wraps if the horse tends to hit the splint area of one leg with the hoof on the other side. Once the condition occurs, the horse must be given enough time to complete the calcification process. From a shoeing perspective, balanced, regular trimming is the best policy to help avoid the problem as well as to minimize stress when the problem exists. It is particularly important that as the riding and conditioning of the young horse progress, hoof balance be maintained through regular hoof care to encourage even weight distribution.

**RINGBONE**    Ringbone is exostosis that occurs at either the coffin joint (joint of the coffin bone, short pastern bone, and navicular bone) or the pastern joint (the joint between the short and long pastern bones) (see chap. 2). The conditions are referred to as low and high ringbone, respectively (fig. 7.15). Exostosis in the pastern area that does not occur at one of the joints is called nonarticular ringbone (fig. 7.16). Like exostosis

**(a)**

**(b)**

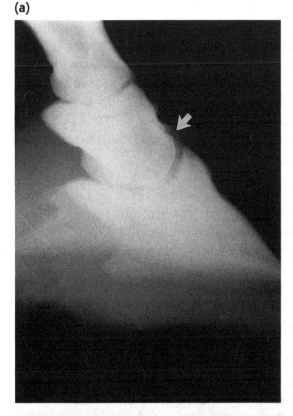

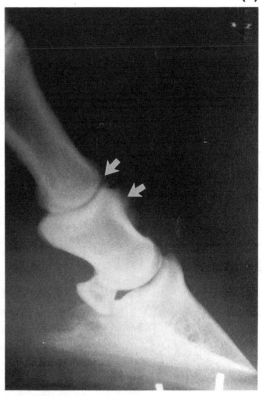

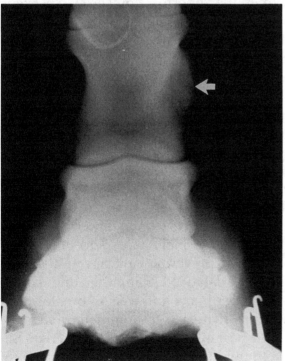

**Figure 7.15** (a) The wispy growth (arrow) is calcification at the joint between the coffin bone and the short pastern bone; when situated here, it is called low ringbone. (b) In high ring-bone, the calcification happens at the joint between the short and long pastern bones (arrow).

**Figure 7.16** An example of nonarticular (not at a joint) ringbone. This may have resulted from a serious wire cut or other trauma to the long pastern bone.

at any site, it begins with a trauma to the surface of the bone. High and low ringbone result from damage to the cartilage surface between the bones. This damage is a consequence of long-term excessive wear at one point of the joint surface caused by faulty conformation and joint flexion beyond the normal range of motion.

In nonarticular ringbone the trauma can be from an injury (a severe wire cut or blow to the pastern). More often, however, it is caused by excessive strain and tearing at ligament attachments and the body's subsequent attempt to repair the damage by forming new bone material. This type of strain is usually associated with hard work combined with poor conformation. In addition, consistently trimming the heels too short, resulting in too low a hoof angle, can place extra strain on some ligament attachments and contribute to the problem.

When the abnormal bony growth of exostosis reaches the point where it interferes with the movement of the bones or the related ligaments, tendons, and nerves, irritation and inflammation result and the horse becomes lame. As a consequence, ringbone can end a horse's useful life because, unfortunately, the possible treatments are limited. Although the condition is easily diagnosed with radiographic pictures, there is no cure. The location, severity, and whether treatment can stop the continuing development of new bone material will determine the animal's fate. Anti-inflammatory drugs prescribed by a veterinarian, frequent, balanced trimming, and shoes that offer support and ease of breakover—therefore requiring less joint movement—are the best options available (see chap. 8), and in mild cases can return an animal to service. In a more severe case, soundness occasionally improves if, through the disease process or by surgery at the pastern joint, the two pastern bones are fused completely.

## NAVICULAR DISEASE

Navicular disease is a painful inflammatory condition affecting any or all of three structures within the hoof—the navicular bone, the navicular bursa, and the deep digital flexor tendon (see chap. 2). Navicular disease is not fully understood, but the general agreement is that it involves stress on the deep flexor tendon, constant excessive shock to the navicular bone, or both. As with many other concussion-related problems, because 60 percent or more of the horse's weight is borne on the front end, it is the front feet and almost never the hind feet that are affected.

One likely contributor to navicular disease is a low hoof angle produced by excessive shoeing intervals or trimming the heels too short, or conformation which results in extra tautness of the deep flexor tendon leading to stress. This low angle also forces the tendon to slide a greater distance over the navicular bursa and bone during a stride, adding to the irritation. At the same time, the three structures are then closer to the ground, with less hoof to protect them and absorb shock. The low-angled hoof position also makes the internal structures like the navicular bursa more accessible to puncture wounds, another potential cause of navicular disease.

An animal with conformationally very steep hoof angles will naturally have more jarring gaits and be prone to develop a variety of concussion-related maladies, including navicular disease. A horse with disproportionately small hooves, unable to dissipate shock adequately, is also at higher risk. This was demonstrated by the relatively high incidence of navicular disease in quarter horses during the time when breeding for tiny "teacup" feet was fashionable.

Irritation or damage can cause changes in the navicular bone as well as calcification of the deep flexor tendon. At this point, diagnosis through X ray is possible (fig. 7.17). Until X-ray-visible calcification/degeneration occurs, diagnosis is based on observing symptoms plus a process of elimination. Pressure, systematically applied with a hoof tester, is often used to locate the source of pain (fig. 7.18). A veterinarian may also inject an anesthetic like carbo-

**Figure 7.17** Calcification of the flexor tendon associated with navicular disease. Normally, because the tendon is a soft structure, it would not show on an X ray at all.

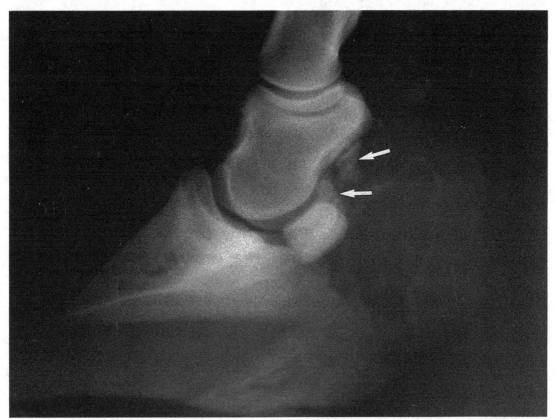

caine into the nerve that innervates the navicular area. If soundness temporarily returns, the source of trouble is narrowed to that area; otherwise navicular disease may be ruled out and the problem looked for elsewhere. This assessment process, however, does occasionally lead to a faulty diagnosis, mistaking other problems as navicular disease. One indication that navicular disease may be present is that horses with the condition are often said to point with one foot, or alternately with both feet. Pointing refers to straightening one foreleg and placing it in front of the other while standing, which removes weight from the foot and eliminates tension on the deep flexor tendon, relieving pressure on the navicular bone and bursa as well.

Treating navicular disease involves special shoeing. Because it is the flexor tendon that pulls the hoof through the breakover portion of the stride, a navicular horse should wear front shoes that make this movement as easy as possible. Rocker-toe

**Figure 7.18** Applying pressure with a hoof tester, trying to locate the source of pain.

or square-toe shoes are well suited for this (chap. 8). Pads for shock absorption may also be in order.

As with other shoeing considerations, one can rarely go wrong by trimming hooves to match the pastern angle. However, there are reports that trimming to an angle higher than normal, which reduces the tautness of the deep flexor tendon, may give some horses relief. This would not be suitable where a naturally steep hoof angle may contribute to the disease.

In some cases, to relieve the pain, a veterinarian may resort to cutting the nerve that innervates the navicular region. Although this can alleviate pain and in some cases return a horse to service, it does not cure the condition. Other measures must be taken to slow the progress of the disease. When an animal has been "nerved," it will no longer be possible to identify further degeneration by judging soundness/lameness, so the risk exists of forgetting that the horse has the problem. This can be significant because without proper care the useful life of the horse is shortened. In particular, quality shoeing designed for navicular disease must be consistently maintained. First-class stable management is also necessary to slow the disease including regular exercise (room to move around is advisable) to encourage good circulation, balanced nutrition, and if possible, living on a soft, springy surface to reduce concussion. The same basic care would be appropriate for any navicular horse, but extra consideration and vigilant hoof care are imperative for the nerved horse because the lack of feeling in the feet can mean that punctures and other injuries go unnoticed.

## LAMINITIS AND FOUNDER

Although the terms laminitis and founder are often used interchangeably, technically they are not the same thing. Laminitis refers to an inflammation of the laminar attachment of the coffin bone to the inside of the hoof (see chap. 2). The word founder, derived from the maritime term that describes a ship sinking, refers to any condition in a horse where the laminae let go of the coffin bone, allowing it to sink or rotate downward.

Considering that the entire weight of the animal is suspended from the inside of the hoof wall by the laminae, it is easy to understand that inflammation or destruction of this tissue is not only painful but a potential disaster. To make matters worse, if conditions are right, a perfectly healthy animal can become extremely sick and permanently disabled in a matter of hours. It is no surprise that horse people are so fearful of laminitis and founder.

The circumstances that start the internal chain of events that culminates in acute laminitis are usually easy to identify. The horse either has been overfed or has broken into the grain-storage area and eaten several times its usual ration; has been given free access to a plush pasture after months of nothing but winter feed; has gotten hot from hard work and, before cooling off, has drunk a large quantity of very cold water; has sustained some type of systemic infection; has been given drugs such as steroids; has eaten a toxic substance; or has recently given birth and did not expel the entire placenta. Overfeeding with grain or on plush pasture is certainly the most common cause of laminitis.

Laminitis is the leading cause of founder,

but not the only cause. Founder can result from a simple mechanical failure. Extreme pounding concussion, like that caused by running a horse on a hard road, can cause more stress than the laminae can withstand. Founder can also occur in a healthy hoof when it must bear excessive weight to make up for a mate that cannot bear weight because of lameness. The healthy hoof's injured laminae become inflamed (laminitis), and separation of coffin bone and hoof wall takes place. In effect, mechanical damage to the laminae has basically the same consequences as the damage caused when laminitis happens first.

In each case internal toxins such as lactic acid are formed, and ultimately blood circulation to the laminae is disturbed. The laminae become swollen, further impeding circulation. The rise in temperature in this region is sufficient to be easily detected by touching the hoof. The impeded blood flow causes a throbbing pulse in the arteries supplying the hoof, which can be felt in the pastern area above the bulbs of the heels. At this point the animal shows signs of lameness.

Acute laminitis is extremely painful. The horse will be reluctant to walk and will often lie down and refuse to get up. When standing, it will typically place both forefeet in front of their normal position and pull the hind feet farther under the body to bear more of the weight.

In a mild case, the horse may be sore for a few days and then return to normal. But if the circulatory disruption is severe enough to damage the laminae, pockets of necrotic (dead) tissue will develop. Abscesses will form, which can further undermine the attachment between laminae and coffin bone.

A change in the relative position of hoof wall and coffin bone often results. The severity of the separation between these structures is the factor that will determine whether the horse's useful life is over. How much separation occurs and in what way it happens are controlled by the amount of laminar tissue destroyed. The size and weight of the animal will also play a role, as will the amount of pull, down and away from the hoof wall, that is naturally placed on the coffin bone by the deep flexor tendon.

Usually the separation happens only in the toe region. In some cases the coffin bone rotates down, out of alignment with the other bones of the lower leg (fig. 7.19). At other times the entire hoof capsule will pivot up at the toe, stretching and distorting above the heels, with the bones remaining basically in their proper relative positions. Either can be seen on an X ray (fig. 7.20), and the severity is defined in degrees of rotation. For example, three degrees of rotation is fairly common in cases of founder, whereas an animal with an angle of fifteen degrees between the coffin bone and hoof wall would have a poor prognosis. In some cases the tip of the coffin bone may point downward far enough to perforate the sole of the foot. In these extreme cases the chances for complete recovery are slim.

Over the many years that humans have cared for horses, countless approaches to treating laminitis have been tried. Horses have been bled, they have been given all sorts of drugs, stood in hot water, cold water, sand, and mud, the soles of their feet have been burned, and all manner of shoes and pads have been applied. Many of the treatments are in opposition to our current understanding of the condition, but all have

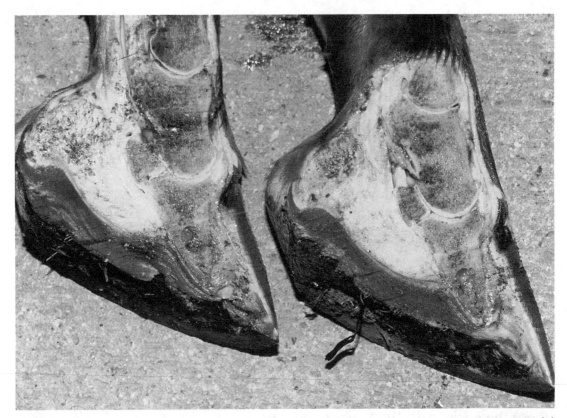

**Figure 7.19**

**Figure 7.20 (a)**

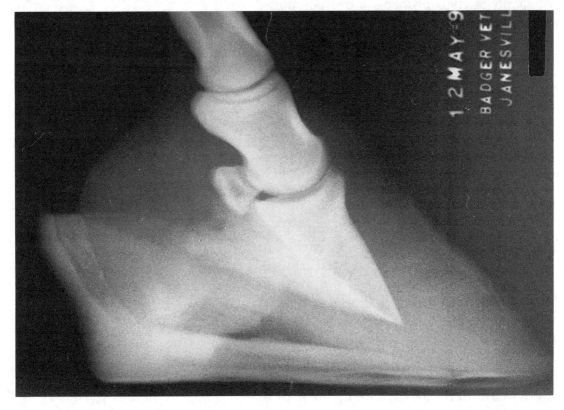

**Figure 7.19** (facing page)A severe separation of both front coffin bones from the inside of the hoof walls, seen during an autopsy. Photo courtesy of Dr. David G. Wilson.

**Figure 7.20** (a) The X ray shows the coffin bone pointing down and away from the hoof wall. (b) A normal hoof: the coffin bone and hoof wall are parallel.

**Figure 7.20 (b)**

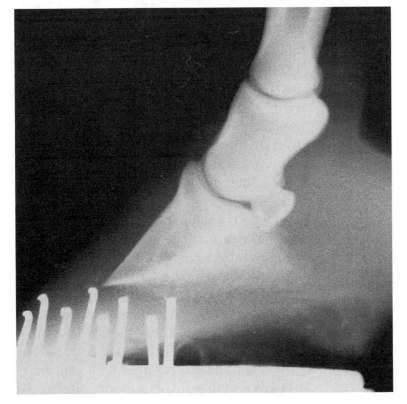

met with success as well as failure. I can only conclude that some horses recover regardless of, or sometimes in spite of, the treatment.

However, in recent years there has been a great deal of research and information exchange regarding laminitis. Great gains have been made, and our understanding has expanded considerably. The well-conceived combined efforts of farrier and veterinarian have resulted in creative, scientifically based treatment approaches. But though the percentage of successes has increased, there is still a discouraging and persistent failure rate. There seem to be animals that will not recover no matter how ingenious the treatment.

A veterinarian should be called as soon as laminitis is suspected or if you find that a horse has gotten into the grain supply. A lot of the damage can be averted with early detection and veterinary care. This care is likely to include a laxative to clean out the digestive tract, anti-inflammatory drugs, and painkillers. This combination slows and mitigates the disease process and allows the horse to stay on its feet. Moving around encourages circulation, which is very important in these cases.

An afflicted animal will often get relief from support applied to the frog. Recently a special pad that can be taped to the foot and has a wedge for frog support has become commercially available. A similar arrangement can be fabricated from flat pads, with triangular frog-sized pieces cut, stacked, riveted together, and placed beneath the frog. The portion of these pads adjacent to the sole is removed or recessed so pressure is only applied to the hoof wall and frog. This gives some of the support offered by heart-bar shoes, as discussed below, and can be used until something more permanent is decided on or the acute attack subsides. I believe these pads will become widely used, because a veterinarian can apply them using only duct tape. In an emergency, a small squashed roll of gauze can be taped to the front portion of the frog. These methods can also be used to support a healthy foot when its mate is unable to bear weight. In any case, during an acute bout with laminitis standard shoes should be taken off so the frog will have more pressure from the ground. A balanced trim may be in order if the hooves have been let go and are in need of attention. Alternating hot and cold foot soaks is also useful to encourage circulation and reduce swelling and inflammation.

Thanks to farrier Burney Chapman of Lubbock, Texas, the heart-bar shoe has been adapted for the treatment of laminitis (fig. 7.21). It works on the principle that

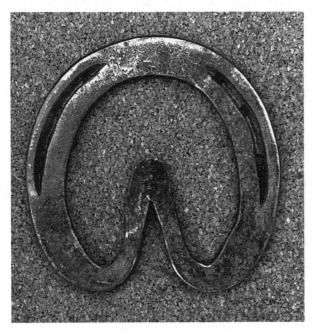

**Figure 7.21** A heart-bar shoe. As a treatment for founder the bar in the middle must apply pressure through the frog to a precise location on the coffin bone. X rays are used to determine the correct position.

supporting the coffin bone by applying pressure through the frog reduces stress on the laminae and can minimize the separation. The pull on the attachment is eased because some weight bypasses the hoof wall and is transferred directly to the bony column without passing through the laminae. In addition, the upward pressure on the coffin bone through the frog and the corresponding downward pull on the hoof wall can sometimes slowly bring the hoof structures into alignment.

If the abscesses that nearly always accompany serious laminitis/founder can heal and healthy laminar growth is encouraged, the attachment between bone and hoof may be reestablished. This may require removing a substantial portion of the front section of the hoof wall so that the abscesses can drain and be treated and dead tissue can be removed. With excellent care, cooperation between veterinarian, farrier, and owner, lots of bandages, and a little luck, the hoof wall will grow down properly attached to the coffin bone.

This treatment for a foundered horse takes about a year, and has two major drawbacks: the vet's time, essential monthly heart-bar resets, medication, and bandages are all very expensive. This cost can be much more than the average owner ever bargained for, maybe more than the horse's market value, even if it were in excellent health. Second, there is no guarantee of success. Many variables should be considered and discussed with a veterinarian and farrier before you undertake such a project. Everyone involved should be fully aware of the time and monetary commitment as well as the odds of success and failure.

In less severe cases, where the separation is minor, with good veterinary and farrier care the horse recovers in a matter of weeks, but the damaged laminae often do not regenerate. The animal has a weakened coffin bone/hoof wall attachment and possibly reduced circulatory function. So, the horse is susceptible to recurrences.

Chronic laminitis of this sort requires extra care and consideration. The horse needs consistent, sensible management and must not be allowed to become overweight, which adds constant stress to the laminar attachment. The amount of use possible without harm will be determined by the severity of the case. With proper care, some animals can return to the same level of activity as before the disease.

As a shoeing concern, a horse with chronic laminitis should be given an easy breakover so that the least possible leverage is exerted on the toe area where the laminae have been damaged. Using standard flat pads must be carefully considered and often is not advisable. When the coffin bone is tilted down in relation to the hoof, small blood vessels might be compressed between bone and pad, which cuts off circulation and can add to the problem. This is also true during treatment of an acute case.

Chronic laminitis can often be identified, even when the animal is sound, by examining the bottom of a horse's foot. Approximately six months after the onset of laminitis, the white line (the line between sole and hoof wall) (see chap. 2, fig. 2.16), which is usually about 1/8 inch wide, will expand, sometimes to over an inch (fig. 7.22). This expansion happens in the toe area and reflects the damage to the laminae. It is wise to check for this when considering a horse for purchase.

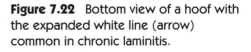

**Figure 7.22** Bottom view of a hoof with the expanded white line (arrow) common in chronic laminitis.

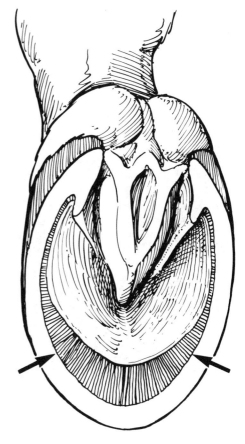

**GENERAL THOUGHTS ON HORSE CARE** When putting together the information for this chapter, it struck me how many problems have, in general, similar care requirements: good stable management, sensible riding habits, correct horseshoeing, balanced (not excessive or deficient) nutrition, and basic veterinary care. The reason is simple: these are the components of responsible horse care even for a sound and healthy animal.

There is a definite cost associated with good horse care, both in time and in money. Failing to consider this when you buy a horse will undoubtedly result in a rude awakening, deficient care, or all too often both. Unfortunately, the biggest loser is usually the horse. For those of us who love horses and derive so much pleasure from them, the extra care is a worthwhile investment. This is not to say that all problems can be avoided, but if we are armed with knowledge and willingness, most can.

# 8

---

# Discovering Choices: Handmade vs. "Keg" Shoes

Many farriers offer hand-forged shoes at a price higher than their usual rate for applying machine-made shoes. In most areas there are some shoers who use mostly (or exclusively) handmade shoes. What's the big deal? Are these shoers just trying to make an extra $10 to $25? What could be so special about handmade shoes over those nice, consistent, one looks the same as the next, right out of the box "keg" shoes that most owners are familiar with? One hundred pounds of these factory-manufactured shoes used to come packed in a keg—hence the name "keg" shoes.

There are many differences between handmade shoes and keg shoes, some subtle and some obvious. Each difference can affect the horse's hooves and performance. It is important to weigh the variables and make a judgment based on the needs of horse and rider. To make an informed choice, an owner must possess some basic knowledge.

When we use a keg shoe, our choices are automatically limited. For instance, the nail holes are prepunched, leaving no way to consider variables like shape or thickness of the hoof wall or to take into account hoof conditions like cracks or missing chunks.

It can also be difficult to accommodate the physiology of the hoof with keg shoes. Weight bearing causes a hoof to expand, and when the foot is lifted it returns to its normal shape (chap. 2). Most often, when bearing weight the heels spread outward. On some hoof shapes, however, the spread is closer to the middle, and so the heels are pulled forward. In both cases the movement can easily be recognized by examining the foot surface of a recently removed shoe. In the heel area there will usually be a groove worn into the steel by repeated movement of the hoof heels (fig. 8.1).

Expansion and contraction of the hoof is an important part of the leg's concussion-absorbing mechanism and also plays a role in moving the deoxygenated blood up the legs and back toward the heart. The most flexible portion of the hoof, called the expansion area, is from the ends of the heels forward to the widest part of the foot. Consequently, much of the shock-absorbing expansion and contraction happens in this area.

Nails will limit expansion and contraction by firmly securing a portion of the hoof wall to the inflexible steel of the shoe. For this reason, a wise horseshoer will rarely drive nails into the expansion area but will instead place them from the widest part forward to the front (toe) of the foot (fig. 8.2). This will allow proper functioning of the hoof. In most cases the design of factory-made shoes does not allow optimum nail placement when using the back nail holes (fig. 8.3). The problem worsens because, to give proper leg support, it is usually best to extend the shoes out past the ends of the heels, which brings that last nail even closer to the heel itself, leaving inadequate expansion room (fig. 8.4).

Also, keg shoes are designed to allow their use regardless of the thickness of the hoof wall. If the nail holes were placed far enough in from the edge of the shoe to correctly accommodate a thick-walled hoof, they would be impossible to use on a thin-walled horse. The manufacturers thus place the holes near the outer edge, which allows shoers to avoid driving nails through sensitive living tissue on all horses. Unfortunately, on a horse with thick hoof walls, the nails penetrate into the outer half instead of near the juncture of the wall and the sole (white line), as is ideal (fig. 8.5). When nails are driven in the outer half of the hoof wall, it is not uncommon for cracks to develop in the hoof wall beneath the clinches.

This does not mean that a proper, safe, and healthy shoeing job can never be accomplished using keg shoes. With care and good judgment they may be appropriate. Here is a list of points that should be considered when using keg shoes:

**Figure 8.1** Repeated expansion and contraction of the hoof wear a groove in the steel shoe.

**Figure 8.3** The handmade shoe (left), does not have nail holes in the expansion area. The heel nails in the keg shoe (right) are behind the widest part of the shoe, within the expansion area.

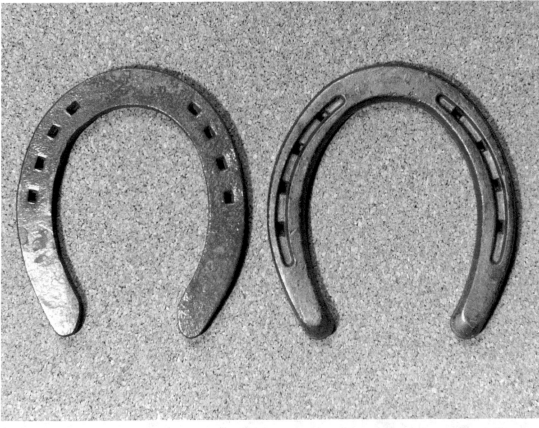

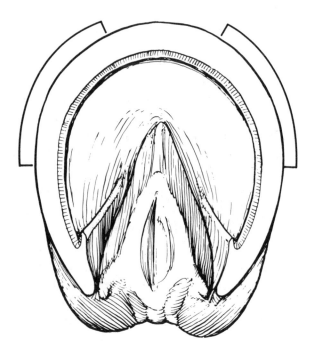

**Figure 8.2** The ideal nailing zone goes back only as far as the widest portion of the hoof. Circumstances such as hoof wall weakness may require varying from this ideal.

**Figure 8.4** (below left) When the keg shoe heels are properly extended beyond the foot, the heel nail holes are even closer to the heel itself. When using a keg shoe, as shown, frequently only the front six nails are in the nailing zone.

**Figure 8.5** (below right) A handmade shoe can be punched to allow nail penetration near the white line even on a thick hoof wall. A prepunched keg shoe has its holes closer to the outside, to be safe (but not necessarily ideal) for every foot.

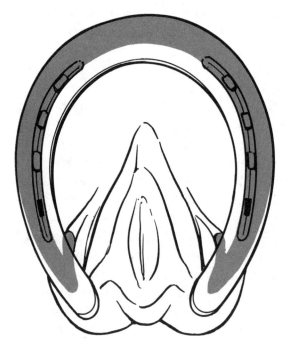

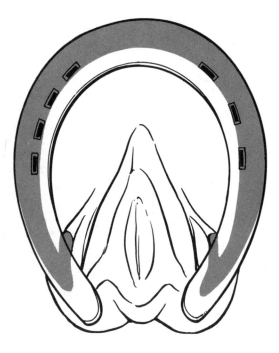

- Will the nail-hole configuration allow for proper expansion, taking into account the shape of the hoof, or can the shoe be safely secured using only the front six nail holes?
- Can the nails be driven to avoid cracks, splits, or missing chunks?
- Will it be possible to catch at least three-fourths of the thickness of the wall when driving the nails?
- Is the standard nail size required by the keg shoes the correct shank thickness for the hoof wall?

If the answer to all the questions above is yes, there is no health-related reason to shun keg shoes. If not, then hand-forged shoes, offering unlimited choice, should be used.

When making a shoe, a farrier can adjust the placement of the nail holes to work around cracks and splits, as well as to account for the thickness of the hoof wall. Whereas keg shoes are prepunched for a common nail size, farriers punching their own nail holes may choose from a variety of possible sizes, depending on the thickness and condition of the hoof wall. In addition, nail holes are usually hand punched on approximately the same angle as the hoof wall (fig. 8.6). The nail pitch that results allows the best possible penetration into sound hoof. Customizing these nailing variables greatly enhances the shoer's ability to securely fasten a shoe with the least risk of damage to the hoof. This flexibility can be very valuable, particularly on horses with thin or fragile hoof horn material.

In addition to considering these important nailing-related variables, the owner and farrier need to develop a clear idea of what the shoeing job is to accomplish. The type of shoes selected can then be matched to the needs of the horse and rider. If a horse is mostly used for trail riding and occasionally goes over a few small jumps, it should not be shod as a jumper (for instance, lightweight, wide-web shoes for extra support and special calks designed for traction when pushing off but minimal drag when landing). Shoeing a trail horse in this fashion will cost more than is necessary and will not produce the desired results. The simpler approach of a longer wearing set of shoes designed for traction appropriate to the terrain would be better suited. The same is true when the goal is to help manage a gait problem. A beautiful shoeing job unsuited to the horse won't resolve the difficulty. The shoe selection should always reflect the riding circumstances and any special needs of the horse.

The multitude of choices provided by handmade shoes can be a big help when trying to solve serious problems as well as when attempting to fine-tune a horse's way

**Figure 8.6** The nail holes of a hand-made shoe (left) are punched to match the angle of the hoof wall. A keg shoe (right) is shown for comparison.

of going. The closer one can come to selecting the best possible size, weight, and style of shoe for the needs of the horse, the better the horse will perform. The improvement can be dramatic, as in correcting a stumbling problem, or subtle, as when an animal becomes a little more comfortable and therefore more relaxed when worked.

A proficient horseshoer with blacksmithing skills can make a set of shoes that precisely fits the needs of any horse. Shoes can be made that are nearly any weight, from very light to very heavy; are extra wide to protect a sensitive sole; have extra weight at the toe, heel, or one side to alter the flight pattern of the leg; have a crease just at the toe, or all the way around for extra traction, or on one side only to pivot the foot slightly; are round on the ground surface to ease breakover; are thicker in the heels to raise the hoof angle; have extended heels to support weak ligaments; or have heel calks or trailers of nearly any size or shape. The list could go on, for the possibilities are limited only by the creativity of the craftsman.

In the hands of a conscientious shoer, many horses can receive healthy and safe service using the quicker to apply and less expensive keg shoes. There are also many horses that do not require any sort of specialized shoeing to meet the needs of their riders. A properly fitted keg shoe is much to be preferred over a poorly made or poorly fitted hand-forged shoe, but the right selection of well-made, properly fitted custom shoes can't be beat for fostering the health and performance of the horse. The more specialized performance requirements are, the greater the difference between hand-forged and keg shoes becomes.

Another point is that keg shoes are made to be malleable (soft and bendable) enough to be shaped over an anvil without being heated. Hand-forged horseshoes are made from bar steel, which is harder and will generally wear longer. For this reason at least part of the extra cost of hand-forged shoes can often be recouped by getting an additional reset or two out of them.

Owners should not hesitate to ask some questions about hand-forged shoes if the subject has not come up before. It may be that they are not available, or the shoer may have assumed that the extra cost would be a deterrent. As always, though, the best bet is to know and understand all the options in order to make informed decisions. Making choices this way can help the owner reach equine-related goals, whether competitive, financial, or simply recreational. Now let's investigate some possible shoe variations and their purposes.

## SPECIALIZED SHOES

By applying good forging skills, it is amazing what creative modifications can be built into a horseshoe. These can be as simple as adjusting the position of the nail holes to accommodate a hoof crack or as complicated as a hinged, padded shoe/brace to aid recovery from a serious tendon problem. Through the use of specially designed shoes, some gait, hoof, and lower-leg problems can be improved or sometimes completely resolved. In addition, shoes can be customized to enhance performance, reduce the stress of movement, and add support.

With this information an owner should be able to recognize some of these options and knowledgeably discuss them with the shoer.

For instance, instead of asking, "What are those extensions sticking out to the side on the hind shoes?" you can ask why the horse was shod with trailers or, better still: "Will the added support of trailers help his cow-hocked stance?"

Horses are individuals, not only in their personalities but in their way of going. A horse's center of gravity, muscular development, coordination, training, and conformation work together to cause it to move in its own distinctive way. This adds to the excitement and challenge of horse ownership and training, equine sports, and choosing horses for breeding. It also adds to the challenge of horseshoeing. Shoeing is an inexact science because a farrier cannot rely solely on formulas to resolve problems. The solution to a gait problem for one horse may not solve a seemingly identical problem on another horse. Success depends on creative application of the fundamental principles, combined with experience, skill, and a little intuition.

A basic tenet of horseshoeing is to try the simplest solution first. Since several approaches to the same problem may work, common sense tells us that the easiest and safest method is the place to begin. If it doesn't work, something else can be tried. In addition, it is generally wise to try one solution at a time, so that it will be clear what action solves the problem. For instance, it would be sensible in most cases to first try plain shoes on a barefoot horse that has become sore. If shoes and pads are used first, we might reach the possibly incorrect conclusion that the pads alleviated the problem, when shoes alone would have had the same result. A pair of pads can add $10 to $20 to the cost of shoeing and slightly increase the risk of a cast shoe.

The following discussion covers some common types of specialized shoes. I recommend learning more by asking questions of the farrier. Most are happy to explain why they chose a certain type of shoe. It is especially important to ask about and understand what increased risks, if any, are associated with special shoes. The chances of a cast shoe may simply be a little greater. Or, as with heel calks, trailers, or extended heels, a horse that kicks may become more of a threat to pasture mates. Being aware of the possible problems, one can take steps to avoid them and still benefit from the specialized shoeing.

## Shoe shape and placement as corrective measures

In a horse with good conformation, a plumb line held in front of the cannon bone will evenly bisect the hoof (fig. 8.7). If it does not, the problem can be found in the lateral balance of the hoof or in one or more of the joints of the leg. In these cases the bony column of the leg is not centered above the hoof and causes the horse's weight to be improperly distributed. If the problem is hoof balance, the solution is as simple as correct trimming. If a joint is poorly conformed, ongoing help may be needed. This horse can be given a foundation that *is* more centered and balanced by putting the shoe where the foot should be (fig. 8.8). This will often require modified nail-hole placement and beveling the shoe's exposed edge so as to decrease the risk of its being stepped off.

A distorted hoof shape can also disturb proper weight distribution (fig. 8.9). In

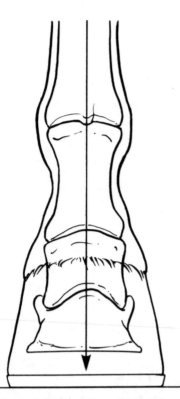

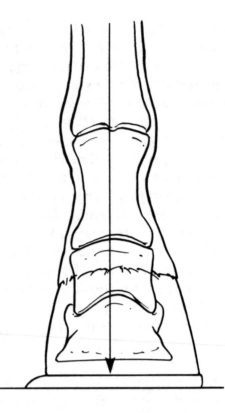

**Figure 8.7** (left) A well-conformed hoof and leg result in even weight distribution centered over the bearing surface.

**Figure 8.8** (right) Shifting shoe placement can be used to move the foundation under the bony column of the leg, even on a poorly conformed limb. Note that the shoe extends to the left, which centers the bony column above the weight-bearing surface.

addition, an asymmetrical toe shape will cause an abnormal breakover, impairing the gait. Working toward correction of such deformities begins with creative sculpturing of the hoof with a hoof rasp. This involves removing as much as is safely possible of the hoof wall that extends beyond a healthy hoof shape. Any missing portions of the weight-bearing foundation can then be compensated for by a shoe that extends to where the hoof would normally be if it were not deformed (figs. 8.10 and 8.11). This simulates a healthy weight-bearing surface and promotes a hoof shape that encourages proper functioning and concussion absorption. It is used for a seriously misshapen hoof or for something as simple as a flat spot on the side of the hoof wall.

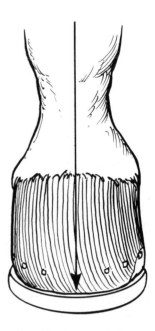

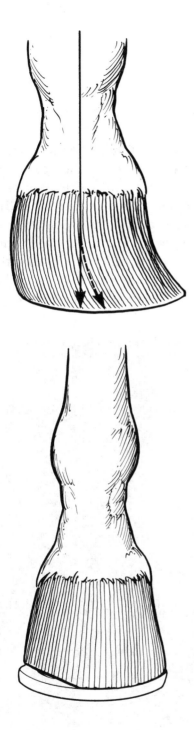

**Figure 8.9** (above left) A wry foot also shifts weight bearing to one side.

**Figure 8.10** (above right) A correctly trimmed and shod wry foot. Note that shoe placement centers weight bearing under the bony column.

**Figure 8.11** (left) Missing hoof wall would encourage faulty breakover. The shoe, however, is used to complete a symmetrical toe shape and encourage efficient movement.

*Risks:* Increased chances of cast shoes. The more of the shoe that protrudes to achieve balance, the greater the risk of casting it.

**Clips** Clips are small steel projections that stick up from the edge of a shoe and lie flush against or seated into the hoof wall (fig. 8.12). They stabilize the position of the shoe and assist the nails in securing shoe to hoof. Clips are commonly used whenever shoes are likely to be lost. Horses with weak hoof walls, heavy or bulky shoes, and horses shod with traction devices that add stress

**Figure 8.12** (a) Shoe with a toe clip, commonly used on front foot; (b) shoe with side clips, commonly used on hind foot.

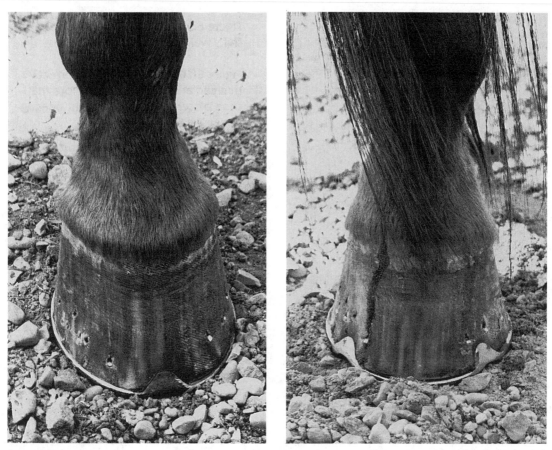

(a)

(b)

to the nails may require clips. A horse that twists its feet as they leave the ground is also a candidate for clips. The twisting motion puts strain on the nails and can loosen shoes.

*Risks:* Clips help hold a shoe on, but if the shoe should be pulled off, each clip is one more hard, upright projection for the animal to step on. Horses with clips should be properly and consistently maintained and never allowed to go long periods between shoeings.

As the name implies, the heels of these shoes stick out farther to the rear than those of normal shoes (fig. 8.13). Frequently the heels are forged so the ends run straight back instead of following the curve of the hoof wall. This type of shoe will add support and protection to a low-angled or "run-under" foot. Run under means that the heels grow forward rather than down (fig. 8.14).

If extended-heel shoes are applied to hind feet, the motion of the hind legs can be slowed as the heels meet the ground and act as a brake. This braking action tends to shorten a horse's stride, which can help prevent it from overreaching or forging. Delaying the hind feet slightly gives the front feet more time to get out of the way.

*Risks:* When reaching with a hind foot to scratch under its chin, a horse might catch its halter with a shoe heel. This would cause it to panic and could be a disastrous and terrifying experience for both horse and owner. For that reason a horse with extended-heel shoes should never be pastured or stalled with a halter on.

## Extended-heel shoes

**Figure 8.13** Extended-heel shoe. The hoof heels would end at the arrows.

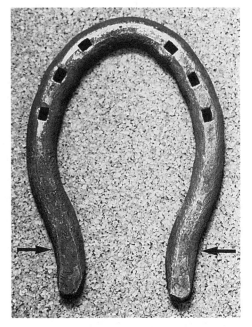

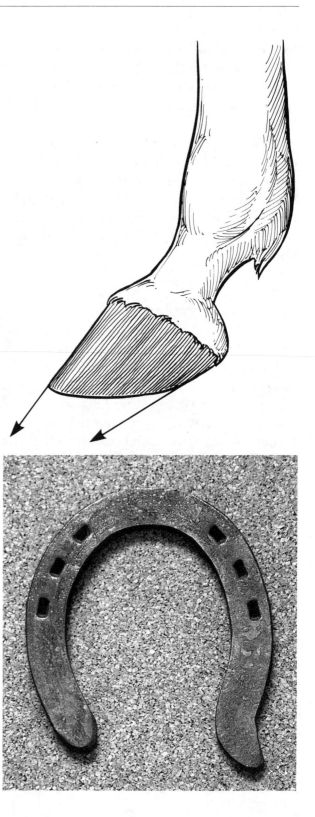

**Figure 8.14** A run-under foot. Note that the heels grow forward rather than on the same angle as the toe. This hoof conformation makes the bulbs of the heels susceptible to bruises and other injuries.

**Figure 8.15** A shoe with a trailer. The trailer is generally used on the lateral (outer) side of the hind foot.

When the heel of the outside branch of a hind shoe is bent to stick out to the side, the shoe is said to have a trailer (fig. 8.15). Trailers offer a lot of lateral support and are especially useful for cow-hocked animals, since they help to support a more correct stance. Combined with a square toe, they help the horse's hind end track straighter.

Some will say that the ideal trailer is a certain length and sticks out at a certain angle, such as 45°. Deferring to what I call the simplest-and-safest rule, trailers should deviate from a normal shoe only as much as it takes to get the desired result.

*Risks:* As with extended heels, a horse shod with trailers should not be left loose with a halter on. Additionally, there is a slightly increased risk of cast shoes since there is more exposed steel to be stepped on by another horse or hooked on a fence.

## Trailers

The shape of square-toe shoes does not follow the hoofline along the front of the toe. Instead, the shoe is flat and the toe of the hoof hangs over by approximately 3/8 inch (fig. 8.16). This has two effects on the horse's movement. It hastens breakover and eases its strain by causing it to happen farther back under the hoof. The hoof can then leave the ground faster. On the front feet this can help a horse that forges or overreaches. The front feet get out of the way before the hind feet can hit them. Square toes can relieve a low-angled animal that typically has extra stress in breaking over. Other modifications such as rocker-toe and rolled-toe shoes have similar results (fig. 8.17).

## Square-toe shoes

**Figure 8.16** A keg shoe, modified to have a square toe. Note that the hoof toe extends over the front of the shoe. Often this portion of the hoof is rasped away. The effect is that the point of breakover is moved back about 3/8 inch.

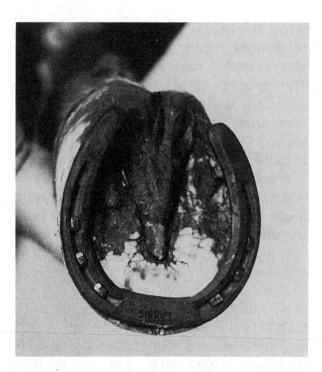

**Figure 8.17** Two other ways to ease breakover: the rocker-toe shoe (left) and the rolled-toe shoe (right). Note that the rocker toe does not have a flat bearing surface for the hoof; the foot is trimmed to match the upward tilt of the rocker toe.

The second gait-altering effect a square-toe shoe can have is to encourage a horse to breakover at the center of the toe, promoting an efficient and straight flight pattern. The straighter the hoof comes off the ground, the straighter the movement through the air and the straighter the landing.

Frequently the tip of the toe is rasped down to the edge of the squared shoe. When done on the hind feet this makes pulled front shoes less likely, because there is less toe there to step on the heels of the front shoes.

*Risks:* When not excessive and when done evenly from one mate to the other, there is no additional risk. Some farriers strongly advocate square or rolled toes on all shod horses. Their argument is that this type of breakover most closely resembles a naturally worn unshod hoof. In my opinion this is not necessary for many horses, but done correctly it does no harm.

## Heel calks and other traction devices

Heel calks are the projections created when the ends of the shoe heels are turned down toward the ground. Basic heel calks are for traction, because the squarish, downward-projecting shoe heels bite into the ground as the foot strikes (fig. 8.18). The exception is walking on pavement, which the calks cannot penetrate. The net result is less surface area in contact with the ground. When the shoes are worn slick on the road surface, a horse will often slip or skate more with calks than without them.

Single heel calks are sometimes used to resolve interference problems because the foot will pivot on the calk when it lands. Whenever a foot's position on the ground is

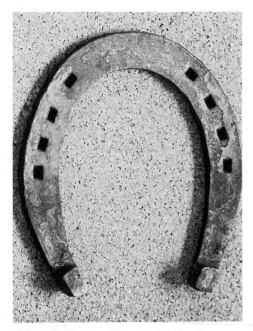

**Figure 8.18** A shoe with heel calks.

**Figure 8.19** A shoe with one creased branch to pivot the foot slightly.

altered it will leave the ground differently, and the flight pattern will be changed as well. The same action can be accomplished to a lesser degree by a flat shoe with a crease on one side only (fig. 8.19). The crease offers more traction than the smooth side, causing a slight pivot as the foot lands. Sometimes this is all the correction needed to solve a problem.

In addition to basic heel calks, specialized calks can perform different functions. For instance, there are calks that do not stop forward motion but offer lateral support and traction for greater thrust when pushing off. These "diamond calks" are often used for jumpers. There are many other variations designed for their jobs, and each type will give different results. Other examples are calks for draft or pulling horses and for traction on snow and ice.

In addition to calks made from the shoe itself, there are studs that can be added to a finished shoe. Studs can vary from tiny nubs to cones an inch long or even longer with very hard tungsten carbide tips that will grip almost any surface, including pavement (fig. 8.20). These are applied by driving them into drilled or punched holes, or studs with threaded bases that can be screwed into corresponding drilled and tapped holes in the shoe heels. The advantage of the screw-in type of studs is that they can be removed when not needed. The disadvantage is that studs, particularly the screw-in type, can add substantially to the cost of the shoeing.

Another way to increase shoe traction besides heel calks and studs is by brazing or welding tungsten carbide chips to the shoe surface. These tiny chunks of high-carbon, extremely hard steel are applied to

**Figure 8.20** A shoe with small studs.

shoes in a matrix of brass or milder steel (fig. 8.21) and are called drill-tech or borium, respectively. Placed across the toe and at each heel of a shoe they offer tremendous traction on nearly any surface including ice. However, the product is quite expensive and time-consuming for the farrier to use.

*Risks:* Trying to pivot a foot that is "stuck" in the ground with calks, studs, or carbide chips can put a lot of extra stress on tendons. The gripping traction of the carbide chips can be particularly hard on a horse's legs because shoeing this way allows nearly no slip or pivot of the shoe at all. For this

**Figure 8.21** A shoe with tungsten carbide chips in a matrix of brass.

reason, traction devices must be selected carefully (if at all) for young horses or those with weak limbs.

Additionally, the extra stress will work at the nails and can eventually loosen them. Clips are commonly used to combat this shoe-loosening tendency. It is also wise to remember that a kicking horse can do a lot more damage when armed with calks, studs, or sharp chips of hard steel.

**Bar shoes** A bar shoe has no opening at the heels like a standard horseshoe (fig. 8.22). There are many variations, depending on the job the shoe is supposed to perform. The three most common are the standard or straight bar shoe, the heart-bar, and the egg-bar. The names reflect the shoes' shape.

An egg-bar shoe (fig. 8.23) is a continuous oval shape. It is used in the same manner as extended-heel shoes. Egg-bars offer great support to the pastern and associated tendons and ligaments. They also help make the sequence of hitting the ground, bearing weight, breaking over, and leaving the ground more fluid and rolling.

The bar on a heart-bar shoe points toward the center of the toe (chap. 7; fig. 7.21). This shoe applies pressure and gives support to the frog. It is used in the treatment and prevention of founder associated with laminitis, discussed in detail in chapter 7. Additionally, applying pressure to the frog can sometimes benefit a horse with contracted heels.

Although each farrier will shape bar shoes a little differently, the basic concept remains the same. A standard shaped shoe is joined at the heels with steel. This is some-

**Figure 8.22**  A farrier has just completed a standard bar shoe as part of the American Farrier's Association journeyman certification test.

**Figure 8.23**  An egg-bar shoe.

times accomplished by welding a piece of steel across the back of a keg shoe. More often though, a shoe is forged from straight bar stock with enough extra length to allow the heels to be bent toward each other and forge-welded into the desired shape.

A basic bar across a shoe will keep even the lightest of shoes from spreading out under the weight of the horse. Some racehorses are shod with bars for this reason.

Bar shoes maintain their shape and spread the weight bearing of the hoof uniformly across the surface of the shoe. This is true even if part of the hoof surface does not meet the shoe. Treating quarter cracks and shoeing a horse that is missing a large chunk of hoof wall are examples of cases when a standard bar shoe would be considered. These applications are discussed in chapter 7.

*Risks:* In general there are no additional risks associated with bar shoes. Heart-bar shoes for founder, however, must be applied with precision, and this should be done only by an experienced farrier with input from an equine veterinarian.

## Weighted shoes

Weighted shoes are simply shoes with a modest amount of extra weight, either all over or on one portion of the shoe. Several ounces may not seem like much for a big, strong horse, but attaching weighted shoes at the ends of such long legs gives the shoes enough leverage to make a difference in the flight pattern. For this reason gaited horses are frequently shod with heavy shoes so they will work harder and pick their feet up higher. The same reasoning will sometimes work with a riding horse that stumbles from laziness and not paying attention to its feet.

Shoes can also be forged so there is more weight at one side, at the toe, or at the heels (fig. 8.24). These purposely unbalanced shoes shift the position of the hoof as it moves through its arc, thereby affecting the flight pattern. Toe weights generally cause a higher arc, heel weights cause the foot to take a longer, sometimes lower stride, and

**Figure 8.24** (left to right): Toe-weight shoe, side-weight shoe, and heel-weight shoe.

side weights are used to modify inefficient gaits, including those associated with interference.

*Risks:* A lot of extra weight can cause strain if the conditioning program does not build up to it.

## Pads

There are five basic reasons to shoe a horse with a pad between hoof and shoe:

- Pads absorb some of the shock as the hoof hits the ground.
- They protect the sole, which can help a horse with chronic sole bruising or a healing injury.
- Thick pads are used on gaited horses to add length and weight to the foot and encourage a more animated gait.
- Anti-snowball pads have a hump on the ground surface that is compressed with weight bearing. When weight is removed and the hump resumes its original position, any snow buildup is pushed out.
- A degree pad that has one end thicker than the other is used to raise or lower the hoof angle.

Pads can cover the entire ground surface of a hoof or be under the shoe only, called a rim pad. Pads are commonly made of plastic or leather, but flat aluminum is occasionally used. When a full pad is applied, some type of hoof packing must fill the space between sole and pad. Otherwise dirt and gravel will fill it and bacteria can breed.

*Risks:* Pads increase the risk of cast shoes. Additionally, a full pad will cause the sole to soften when moisture is trapped, as happens to our skin under a Band-Aid.

When pads are removed, care should be taken to avoid bruising until the sole hardens and toughens.

In conclusion, note that many problems can be resolved or avoided with balanced trimming and correctly fitted flat shoes. With this combination, efficient movement is limited only by conformation, conditioning, and the rider's skill. This approach also avoids creating the internal stress associated with some types of specialized shoeing. Nevertheless, if the horse competes in an equine discipline, there is some specialized shoeing approach that exactly matches the animal's needs. A little extra support, modified traction, or gait-enhancing shoes may offer an edge in competition. If the horse is simply ridden for pleasure, specialized shoeing is needed only to solve specific problems. Examples are to give extra traction on ice or rocky terrain, to help heal or prevent injuries or disease conditions, or to correct interference.

Before one undertakes gait correction through shoeing, it must be established that the problem does not rest elsewhere. No shoeing job can overcome difficulties associated with improperly fitted tack or the rider's poor balance. One interesting example is that a horse with plugged tear ducts tends to stumble. It would be unfortunate to spend time and money trying different shoeing approaches to solve a problem a veterinarian could resolve in ten minutes.

When considering shoeing as an approach to change a horse's way of going, one must also remember an old saying: A miss is as good as a mile. In other words, even if a gait looks inefficient, there is no interference problem unless one leg is hitting another. Coming close doesn't count—it is just that horse's unique way of moving. Unless the gait hinders equine activities or the horse is uncomfortable, it is not a problem. Don't shoe a horse to solve a difficulty it doesn't have.

# 9

# An Inside
# View

The previous chapters have examined the mechanics of horseshoeing. To round out one's understanding of the profession as a whole, as a consumer or as someone considering horseshoeing as a career, requires two more things: a brief look at how (and why) someone becomes a farrier, and some insight into the prices charged for shoeing services.

Horseshoeing is not a particularly glamorous profession. The job is physically and mentally demanding, and it can take years for a business to generate a good income. At times it is even dangerous. That being said,

it may be difficult to understand why anyone would choose shoeing as an occupa-
tion. Setting out to write this chapter certainly is not the first time I have pondered
this question. I am especially prone to
examine my chosen profession at the end of
a difficult day. On these days I am battered,
bruised, scraped, and cut by misbehaving
horses. I have accomplished less than I set
out to do. Some of what I achieved didn't
quite meet my expectations, and even when
something came out exceptionally well, the
other people involved didn't recognize the
effort, let alone appreciate it.

On the other hand, sometimes things do
work out as planned, and the job comes out
the way I anticipated. The battle of wills
with an uncooperative horse goes my way
without any injuries, and the animal real-
izes that it's not scary to stand and allow me
to do my work. On these days I get reports
about the ribbons a client has won and
about how wonderfully a lame horse has re-
sponded to the therapeutic shoes I applied.

There is more to it, though, than the good
days versus the bad days. There is the
sense of independence, the challenge, and
the satisfaction of the creative process.
Another important part for me is that the
combination of precision work, physical
exertion, and the unpredictability of horses
discourages being preoccupied with other
matters. The horses don't allow the job to
get boring, because to maintain safety shoers
must not only watch and listen but also pay
attention with their whole bodies: feeling
the horse's subtle (and not so subtle) movements and tensions. I like to compare this
with the meditative idea of living in the
present, similar to what's needed for riders
to be in perfect rapport with their mounts.

The rider about to attempt a six-foot jump is not thinking about last week's flat tire or upcoming tax returns.

Just as riders cannot relax and be in harmony with their horses until they lose their clumsiness with the equipment and are comfortable with the fundamentals of riding, so it is with the horseshoer. Learning the job takes years and is the unavoidable way those wishing to excel must pay their dues.

For instance, the horseshoer starting a business usually has to accept less desirable clients in order to build skills and a reputation. In this context, less desirable means poor working conditions and uncooperative horses. In addition, there is no formal educational structure to help a beginner advance beyond mere fundamentals to understanding and mastering the finer points of the trade.

This initial period is a major obstacle that in many cases is never overcome. As a result, the vast majority of farrier-school graduates are not shoeing professionally after five years. This does not mean a new shoer will have undesirable accounts exclusively, but when starting out you must take what's available in order to have horses to work on so you can begin developing an income base and hone skills. Novice shoers must use good judgment, however, to avoid placing themselves at undue risk with dangerous animals and unsafe barn conditions.

## EDUCATION

There are about sixty schools in North America that offer training in horseshoeing. They vary in course length from two weeks to one year, but most courses last between eight and sixteen weeks. One should understand that these schools give only a foundation for continued learning. It requires motivation to further one's education and avoid mediocrity (or worse). In addition to the length of the course, a prospective student should investigate and compare several other variables when choosing a school. These include the qualifications of the instructors; the ratio of teachers to students; the time spent actually working on horses; and the time spent practicing forgework. A list of horseshoeing schools is provided in appendix A.

The fastest and most efficient way to gain knowledge and skill is first to attend one of these horseshoeing schools and then to spend time working with an experienced shoer. At school you should be introduced to anatomy and physiology, an overview of lameness problems, basic forgework, and the tools and how they are used (including supervised practice time), as well as receiving instruction on basic horseshoeing principles. This background increases the likelihood of later arranging some type of learning situation with a skilled shoer.

Taking time to teach slows down a farrier's work. As a result, even informal, short-term apprenticeships can be difficult to secure, since many farriers see little advantage to spending time with a beginner. Even with the foundation provided by a school, it could easily be weeks before a student would no longer slow down the workday of an experienced farrier. Consequently it is difficult enough for graduates, let alone nongraduates, to begin their education by working with a skilled craftsman.

Important additional sources of information and training are workshops and clinics sponsored by many local farriers' associations, of which there are over forty in North America. Many top farriers spend part of their time sharing their expertise in such workshops. In addition to learning from the clinician, joining an association gives novices the opportunity to meet more experienced shoers who can answer some of their questions and offer advice on difficult cases. This type of continuing education is also the best way for any shoer to stay abreast of new technology and developments in the industry. The American Farrier's Association can provide information about local associations and about activities for farriers (appendix B). By attending seminars and studying up-to-date information provided by magazines like the *American Farriers Journal* (published by the Laux Company, Maynard, MA), and *Anvil* magazine (published by Rob Edwards, Georgetown, CA), many learners bypass apprenticeships, but I still recommend a one-on-one learning situation, if possible, as the fastest, safest way to prepare for a career in shoeing.

## INCOME POTENTIAL AND COMPETITION

When you consider starting any business, it is prudent to examine its money-making potential. In addition, you should be prepared for an initial period of little or no income, starting with the time spent in school and continuing until a client base is developed. In my opinion, however, wherever there are horses there is usually room for a responsible and skilled professional. It is a matter of finding one's niche and developing a good reputation in the community.

According to the American Horse Council, there are nearly ten million horses in the United States, and many areas do not have enough skilled shoers to care for the local population. However, a better feel for each area can be obtained by talking to local people. If many of the local farriers are refusing new customers and it takes weeks for owners to get someone to do work, it is a good indication of the need for additional trained shoers.

In some cases some owners in an area may be stuck with a shoer who offers poor service, low-quality work, or both. Given an alternative, they would gladly give someone else their accounts. Sound business practices, a responsible attitude, and good shoeing skills diligently applied in the right geographic area can bring an independent life style and a satisfactory income.

## PRICES

Some years back, while living in southwestern Missouri, I was working on a horse that a kind woman had saved from terribly neglectful circumstances. Each time I saw this animal it was looking better and, unfortunately, getting harder to handle—one might say, fatter and sassier.

On one occasion the woman's friend from town happened to be visiting when I did my work, so the two women talked while my customer held the lead rope. Well, I wrestled and cajoled a bit, but I got the job done. Still perspiring and a little out of breath, I handed over my bill. Glancing at the bill, the friend began to laugh. She apologized for her unexpected outburst and explained that just that morning she had paid more for a manicure.

As one might imagine, that incident got me thinking. My prices had originally been set to attract new accounts and to be competitive in my area. Not having much business background, I didn't really know if my fee schedule was equitable. How much to charge seemed worth investigating. I decided that I first needed to know what my expenses were, so I made a list. The following revised list includes items that will not apply to every horseshoer. Most, however, will have the majority of these expenses, and some will have them all.

- Vehicle expenses
    Work-truck payment
    Tires and maintenance
    Gasoline
- Insurance
    Health and accident insurance
    Disability insurance
    Business liability insurance
    Commercial vehicle insurance
    Retirement plan
- Supplies
    Shoes
    Steel
    Nails
    Hand tools
    Power tools
    Blacksmithing equipment
    Propane or coal
    Pads/leather
    Hoof packing
    Fly spray
    Hoof sealant
    Miscellaneous items and
        equipment
- Education
    Initial schooling investment

Seminars/workshops
(tuition & travel)
Trade journals
Books
Annual convention
•   Miscellaneous
Office supplies
Association dues
Telephone
Taxes and FICA
Tax accountant
Computer for customer records
& billing
Advertising (newspaper ads,
business cards)

Like any other business, there is an initial investment and myriad ongoing expenses that must be maintained in order to turn on the lights and open the door (or the tailgate). Additionally, many horseshoers maintain a shop at home for storage and to do forging projects like making shoe blanks in advance. This means doubling up on some tools.

One other part of the picture is that for every hour spent actually shoeing horses, another half hour or so is invested for which no fees are charged. This includes driving time, inventory handling, maintaining the truck and other equipment, answering questions on the phone, office work (setting appointments, bookkeeping, etc.), making shoes, and staying abreast of new developments in the trade, as well as taking care of the occasional lost shoe (sometimes at no charge). Depending on the way the business is run, the number of customers, and the rates that are charged, it can cost as little as 40 percent or as much as 75 percent of the fees charged just to operate the business.

A portion of the horse-owning public and some shoers do not realize how much it costs to operate a horseshoeing business. For instance, it is still possible in some areas to get a horse shod for about $20. This is surprising, because the shoer has about $7 invested in just the shoes, nails, and wear on a rasp. This doesn't account for gasoline (or the truck to put it in) or any of the other expenses listed above.

The shoer charging low rates will have to make some compromises to stay in business. The expense of stocking supplies and purchasing tools will have to be minimized, which means fewer choices in the field and perhaps making do with something that is not quite right. A greater problem is that more horses must be shod to make a living, allowing less time per animal as well as less unscheduled time open to deal with emergencies. Fewer choices, lower-quality equipment, long hours, and less time spent per job seem likely to lead to diminished work quality. "You get what you pay for" has become an old saying because of the truth it contains.

The *American Farriers Journal*, a trade journal for the industry, conducted a survey in 1989 of 493 horseshoers nationwide. The average prices reported were as follows: for a trim, $14.37; for shoeing a horse on all four feet with keg shoes, $40.70; with basic hand-forged shoes, $54.51. Prices were generally higher in the northeastern United States, with no one area consistently the lowest.

When considering these figures, it's important to keep in mind that they represent an average. They include farriers fresh out of school as well as top-notch shoers who have refined their skills over many years. They also do not differentiate between rural and metropolitan areas. In some cases the spread between the lowest and highest charges reported for the same service was great. For instance, the nationwide average for resetting four shoes was $34.14. For this service the lowest price reported was $15 and the highest was $125. However, high rates are not a guarantee of high quality any more than low rates guarantee poor craftsmanship. Quality must be judged on its own merit.

The foregoing survey assessed the cost of basic shoeing with keg and handmade shoes. It is even more difficult to generalize about the cost of specialized forge work. Some shoers charge a flat rate for shoeing no matter what, with no additional cost for custom work. This allows them to shoe each horse in the way that seems most appropriate without needing to justify or explain extra charges. Often a set charge is assessed for the specific task—for example, per clip or heel calk. Sometimes, particularly when complicated therapeutic shoes are involved, the charges may be based on time and materials. Horseshoers set their own policies and certainly should be willing to explain them clearly to their customers.

Another factor that can affect the cost of horseshoeing is specialization. Every competitive equine activity has farriers who make it their business to understand the finer points of the discipline. For instance, hunter/jumpers, endurance racers and competitive trail horses, western performance horses, dressage horses, and many of the various breeds, as well as each type of racehorse (thoroughbred, quarter horse, and standardbred) all have horseshoeing specialists, highly skilled in their care. There are also those who dedicate themselves to therapeutic shoeing, dealing with problems and lameness.

Each discipline has its own subtleties and nuances that must be mastered. In some cases special rules governing horseshoeing must be followed; for example, several breeds have shoe weight limits as well as restrictions on pads that one must adhere to or risk being disqualified from shows. Shoers who devote years to refining their skill in one particular area deserve to receive a greater return from those who benefit from their expertise.

In recent years the level of cooperation and information sharing between horseshoers has risen enormously. For this reason, there always seem to be shoers willing to give helpful information to those considering horseshoeing as a trade. The local farriers' association is also a good place to seek input (see appendix B).

Remember that if you do not enjoy your work, no amount of money can make up for it. This seems particularly true for this profession, because the horses will usually respond to a negative attitude in a negative way. Hence, what initially seems unpleasant can get worse. Fortunately, for those who like the work and apply themselves, their expertise grows, as does a client list of interesting and committed horse people. In these cases the opposite occurs: it gets better and better.

# Appendix A

# North American Farrier Schools

ALABAMA

Lookout Mountain School
   of Horseshoeing
Rt. 8, Box 277
Gadsden, AL 35901
(205) 546-2036

ARIZONA

Tucson School of Horseshoeing
2230 North Kimberlee Road
Tucson, AZ 85749
(602) 749-5212

VisionQuest Learning Center
3571 East River Road
Tucson, AZ 85718
(602) 299-8993

Western's School of Horseshoeing
2801 West Maryland Avenue

Phoenix, AZ 85017
(602) 242-2560

CALIFORNIA

California Polytechnic State University
Horseshoeing Unit
San Luis Obispo, CA 93407
(805) 756-2409

California State Polytechnic University
3801 West Temple Avenue
Pomona, CA 91768
(714) 869-2224

Gavilan College
5055 Santa Teresa Boulevard
Gilroy, CA 95020
(408) 842-8411

Hacienda La Puente Adult Education
   Farrier Program
15336 East Proctor Avenue
City of Industry, CA 91746

Lassen College
714-825 Sagebrush Boulevard
Susanville, CA 96130
(916) 254-6795

Merced College
3600 M Street
Merced, CA 95340
(209) 383-6250

Porterville Horseshoeing School
Elk Grove Campus
11120 Bradley Ranch Road
Elk Grove, CA 95624
In state: (916) 689-4900
or 689-4460
Out of state: (800) 233-1444

Sierra Horseshoeing School
Rt. 1, Rocking K
Bishop, CA 93514
In state: (619) 872-2505
Out of state: (800) 443-2848

Valley Vocational Center
359 East Proctor Avenue
City of Industry, CA 91744
(818) 968-4638, ext. 4605

COLORADO

Pikes Peak Community College
1528 Turner Road
Colorado Springs, CO 80918
(719) 598-5569

FLORIDA

Florida School of Horseshoeing
P.O. Box 423
Belleville, MI 48111
(313) 697-9331

IDAHO

Sharp's Shoeing Forge
423 Confederate Drive
Salmon, ID 83467
(208) 756-2808

ILLINOIS

Equine Educational Services
P.O. Box 413, Dept. HS
O'Fallon, IL 62269-0413
(618) 632-7921

Midwest Horseshoeing School
2312 South Maple Avenue
Macomb, IL 61455
(309) 833-4063

KANSAS

Colby Community College
1255 South Range
Colby, KS 67701
(913) 462-3984, ext. 250

KENTUCKY

Kentucky Horseshoeing School
P.O. Box 120
Mount Eden, KY 40046
In state: (502) 738-5257
Out of state: (800) 626-5359

MICHIGAN

Michigan School of Horseshoeing
P.O. Box 423
Belleville, MI 48111
(313) 697-9331

Wolverine Farrier School
7690 Wiggins Road
Howell, MI 48843
(517) 546-1429

MINNESOTA

Minnesota School of Horseshoeing
6250 Front Street, NW
Anoka, MN 55303
(612) 421-5750

MISSOURI

Northwest Missouri State University
Agriculture Department
Maryville, MO 64468
(816) 562-1659

MONTANA

Montana State University
Bozeman, MT 59715
(406) 994-5578

NEW JERSEY

Far Hills Forge
P.O. Box 703
Far Hills, NJ 07931
(201) 766-5384

NEW MEXICO

Tucumcari Area Vocational School
P.O. Box 1143
Tucumcari, NM 88401
(505) 461-4413

Tucumcari Farrier School
P.O. Box 36
Tucumcari, NM 88401
(505) 461-2942

NEW YORK

Cornell University
Department of Clinical Studies
Ithaca, NY 14850
(607) 253-3127

OKLAHOMA

Oklahoma Farrier's College, Inc.
Rt. 2, Box 88
Sperry, OK 74073
In state: (918) 288-7221
Out of state: (800) 331-4061

Oklahoma Horseshoeing School
3000 North Interstate 35
Oklahoma City, OK 73111
In state: (405) 424-3842
Out of state: (800) 538-1383

Oklahoma State Horseshoeing School
Rt. 1, Box 28-B
Ardmore, OK 73401
(405) 223-0064

OREGON

Linn-Benton Community College
630 NW Seventh
Corvallis, OR 97330
(503) 758-1736

TENNESSEE

State Blacksmith and Farrier School
Rt. 1, Box 144
Bloomington Springs, TN 38545
(617) 653-4341 or 653-4440

TEXAS

Gulf Coast Farriers School
2701 Mustang Road
Alvin, TX 77511
(713) 331-4092

North Texas Farriers School
P.O. Box 666
Mineral Wells, TX 76067
(817) 325-5202

Sul Ross State University
P.O. Box C-110
Alpine, TX 79830
(915) 837-8210

Texas Horseshoeing School
P.O. Box 188
Scurry, TX 75158
(214) 452-3159

Texas School of Farrier Science
P.O. Box 127
Peaster, TX 76074
(817) 594-6710 or 599-3173

UTAH

Utah School of Horseshoeing
429 South Angel
Layton, UT 84041
(801) 544-1996

VIRGINIA

Eastern School of Farriery
P.O. Box 1368
Martinsville, VA 24114
(703) 638-7908


WASHINGTON

Northwest School of Horseshoeing
P.O. Box 31
College Place, WA 99324
(509) 522-HOOF (4663)


South Puget Sound Community
    College
2011 Mottman Road SW
Olympia, WA 98502
(206) 753-3447


Walla Walla Community College
500 Tausick Way
Walla Walla, WA 99362
(509) 527-4291


WEST VIRGINIA

Meredith Manor International
    Equestrian Centre
Rt. 1, Box 76
Waverly, WV 26184
(304) 679-3128


WISCONSIN

Gateway Technical Institute
400 South Highway H
Elkhorn, WI 53121
(414) 741-6100


University of Wisconsin at River Falls
Summer Horse Institute
River Falls, WI 54022
(715) 425-3704 or (507) 545-2299


WYOMING

Laramie County Community College
1400 East College Drive
Cheyenne, WY 82001
(307) 634-5853


Northwest Community College
Equestrian Studies Program
Powell, WY 82435
(307) 754-6610


ALBERTA, CANADA

Olds College
Olds, Alberta TOM 1PO
(403) 556-8251


BRITISH COLUMBIA, CANADA

Kwantlen College
Langley Campus
P.O. Box 9030
Surrey, British Columbia
V3T 5H8
(604) 533-2515


NOVA SCOTIA, CANADA

Atlantic Farrier School
RR 3, Saltsprings
Pictou County, Nova Scotia BOK 1PO
(902) 925-2219


ONTARIO, CANADA

Canadian School of Horseshoeing
RR 2
Guelph, Ontario N1H 6H8
(519) 824-5484


Kemptville College of Agricultural
    Technology
Kemptville, Ontario KOG 1JO
(613) 258-3411

Seneca College of Applied Arts and
  Technology
RR 3, Dufferin Street North
King City, Ontario LOG 1KO
(416) 833-3333

This list was provided by the American Farrier's Association. No representation of the validity or quality of any school or program is intended. Interested individuals should do careful research before participating in any course.

## Appendix B

# Farriers' Associations and Activities

For information about national and local farrier activities, or to locate the nearest regional farriers' association, write or call:

American Farrier's Association
Kentucky Horse Park
4089 Iron Works Pike
Lexington, Kentucky  40511
(606) 233-7411

# Glossary

**Abscess:** A localized collection of pus surrounded by inflamed tissue.

**Anatomy:** The study of the position and structure of the body's parts.

**Anvil:** A heavy metal block used for support when hammering metal to change its shape.

**Bar shoe:** A shoe that has no opening at the heels.

**Bars:** The part of the hoof wall that is bent inward toward the frog at the heel on each side and extends toward the center of the sole.

**Base-narrow stance:** A stance in which the hooves are closer together than the shoulders.

**Base-wide stance:** A stance in which the hooves are farther apart than the shoulders.

**Bowlegged:** Having the legs curved outward at the knees.

**Breakover:** The action in which the hoof pivots over the toe as it leaves the ground when the horse is moving forward.

**Bulb:** The fleshy, rounded upper portion of the heel of a horse's foot.

**Bursa:** A padlike sac filled with fluid, usually found near joints in connective tissue. It has a synovial membrane lining and acts as a friction reducer.

**Calf-kneed:** Having the legs misaligned so that the bones above the knee are behind the bones below the knee.

**Calcification:** The introduction of calcium on or into any tissue, other than normal bone growth.

**Calks:** Downward projections at the heels of a shoe that offer extra traction.

**Cannon bone:** The long bone extending

from the knee or hock to the fetlock.

**Carpal:** One of the bones making up the knee joint.

**Cartilage:** A translucent elastic tissue that covers the bone ends meeting within a joint.

**Cast shoe:** A shoe that is pulled off between shoeings.

**Clinch:** A small, flat square of metal made by folding down a nail stub that has emerged from the side of the hoof. The clinches play a major role in securing shoe to hoof.

**Clinch block:** A small block of metal that is held against each nail stub while the nail is struck one last time to seat the head in the shoe. This locks the nail in place by forming the initial bend of a clinch. Some shoers use the top of their pull-offs for this part of the shoeing operation.

**Clincher:** A jawed tool for bending the stubs of shoeing nails to form the small metal squares (clinches) that secure the shoe to the hoof. Also called clinching tongs.

**Clips:** Thin triangular projections that stick up from the edge of a shoe and lie flush against or seated into the hoof. Clips help take stress off the nails and stabilize the position of the shoe.

**Coffin bone:** One of the bones enclosed within the hoof, attached to the front two-thirds of the hoof wall and connected at the back to cartilage.

**Conformation:** The structure of a horse as compared with an ideal for efficient functioning.

**Connective tissue:** A material composed of spindle-shaped cells with interlacing processes that pervades, supports, and binds together other tissues and forms ligaments and tendons.

**Contracted heels:** A condition in which the heels are drawn too close together, preventing proper expansion of the hoof and putting pressure on the soft structures of the foot.

**Corn:** A deep bruising of the sole usually seen between the hoof wall and the bars.

**Coronary band:** The fleshy ring around the top of the hoof from which the hoof wall grows. Commonly called the coronet.

**Corrective shoeing:** Trimming, application of shoes, or both, designed to improve or eliminate a stance or gait flaw.

**Cow-hocked:** Having the hocks, closer together than both the hips and the fetlocks.

**Cracked heels:** See Greased heels.

**Crossties:** A common restraint method consisting of two ropes or chains fastened to opposite sides of a barn aisle or stall that can be secured to each side of a horse's halter.

**Dished hoof:** A distortion of the toe portion of the hoof in which the wall is concave.

**Dubbing the toe:** Rasping off part of the hoof wall that hangs over the front of the shoe. This is done to make the shoe appear to fit correctly.

**Egg-bar shoe:** A shoe made in a continuous oval shape to support the pastern and its associated tendons and ligaments.

**Epiphyseal plate:** See Growth plate.

**Equine:** Of or pertaining to horses.

**Exostosis:** The buildup of calcium on a bone as a repair measure when the bone's outer skin (periosteum) has been damaged or irritated. Also, a lump caused by this process.

**Expansion area:** The flexible part of the hoof from the ends of the heels forward to the widest part of the foot.

**Extended-heel shoe:** A shoe on which the heels project farther in the rear than on a normal shoe.

**Farrier:** A horseshoer, usually one who works with steel to make horseshoes;

from the Latin word *ferrum,* "iron."

**Fetlock:** The joint where the long pastern bone and the cannon bone meet, incorporating the proximal sesamoid bones.

**Finish work:** Shoeing operations performed after the shoe is nailed on, including folding down and smoothing the clinches, filling nail holes, and applying sealant.

**Flared hoof:** A distortion of a side of the hoof in which the wall spreads outward at the bottom.

**Forge:** A furnace used to heat metal. While hot, the metal is soft and bendable, which allows its shape to be easily changed by hammering.

**Forging:** A gait flaw in which the bottom of a front foot contacts the toe of a hind foot.

**Founder:** A condition in which the laminae become detached from the coffin bone, allowing it to sink or rotate downward.

**Frog:** The resilient, flexible, wedge-shaped structure on the bottom of a horse's foot.

**Gait:** A horse's unique way of going. Also, any of the various movements such as walk, trot, and canter.

**Greased heels:** A dermatitis that affects the soft skin at the back of the pastern above the heel bulbs, causing scabs that may crack and bleed. Also called scratches.

**Growth plate:** The thin cartilage layer near the ends of bones from which growth occurs in a young horse. Also called epiphyseal plate.

**Heart-bar shoe:** A shoe with a bar extending from the rear toward the tip of the frog to apply pressure and give support.

**Hoof angle:** The angle formed by the line of the front of the hoof relative to the ground surface.

**Hoof gauge:** See Protractor.

**Hoof knife:** A tool with a small, sharp curved blade used for trimming the sole and frog of a horse's foot.

**Hoof pick:** A tool with a bent screwdriver-shaped blade used for cleaning dirt and debris from the bottom of the hoof.

**Hoof tester:** A large-jawed diagnostic tool used for locating the source of pain by systematically applying pressure to a hoof.

**Hoof wall:** The horny material that makes up the outer part of the hoof and is the primary contact with the ground.

**Hoof stand:** The pedestal used to support a horse's foot in a forward position while sculpting the hoof and performing the finish work of the shoeing operation. Some shoers prefer to hold the foot on their knee instead.

**Horn tubules:** Thin vertical tubes, cemented together, that make up the hoof wall.

**Interference:** A flawed gait, characterized by one or more legs being struck by another leg during movement.

**Joint:** The meeting place of two or more bones.

**Keg shoes:** Machine-made shoes available in stock sizes, as opposed to hand-forged shoes.

**Knock-kneed:** Having the legs curved inward at the knees.

**Laminae:** The thin folds of vascular tissue that attach the coffin bone to the inside of the hoof wall.

**Laminitis:** An inflammation of the laminae that attach the coffin bone to the inside of the hoof.

**Lateral balance:** Side-to-side balance that is present when the weight borne by a leg is as evenly distributed around the hoof as conformation permits.

**Ligament:** Tough band of tissue that connects bones to one another.

**Matrix:** The protein framework within

which calcium salts are deposited to form bone.

**Navicular bone:** A boat-shaped bone enclosed within the hoof and articulating with the back of the coffin bone and bottom rear portion of the short pastern bone.

**Navicular disease:** An inflammatory condition affecting the navicular bone, the navicular bursa, and the deep digital flexor tendon.

**Nerving:** Cutting a nerve to relieve pain.

**Nippers:** A jawed tool with sharp cutting edges used for trimming the hoof wall.

**Offset knees:** Legs that are misaligned so that the bones above the knees are positioned outside those below the knees.

**Ossification:** Normal bone growth caused by the introduction of calcium salts into the protein matrix produced at the growth plates.

**Osteoblast:** A specialized cell that secretes protein to form the bone matrix.

**Osteoclast:** A specialized cell that dissolves protein in the bone matrix, releasing calcium into the bloodstream.

**Over-at-the-knee:** Having the legs misaligned so that the bones above the knee are forward of the bones below the knee.

**Overreaching:** Striking the heels of the front feet with the toes of the hind feet.

**Pad:** A piece of plastic, leather, or aluminum placed between the hoof and the shoe to protect the sole and help absorb shock.

**Pastern:** The part of the horse's leg extending from the fetlock to the top of the hoof.

**Periosteum:** The membrane of connective tissue covering a bone.

**Physiology:** The study of the function of the body's parts.

**Pointing:** Straightening one foreleg and placing it in front of the other while standing. Commonly seen in horses with navicular disease.

**Pricking:** Penetrating the sensitive living tissue inside the hoof with a nail.

**Protractor:** An instrument that measures the hoof angle in degrees. Also called a hoof gauge.

**Pull-offs:** A thick-jawed tool used for prying horseshoes from a horse's hooves. Some pull-offs can also be used for cutting nails.

**Quarters:** The sides of the hoof wall, between the heel and the toe.

**Radiograph:** A photograph produced by exposing highly sensitive film to X rays or gamma rays.

**Rasp:** A large file that has one rough side with large teeth and one smoother side with a finer cutting surface, used for trimming and shaping a horse's hooves.

**Reset:** An operation in which the shoer removes a set of shoes, trims the hooves, and then replaces the same shoes. The amount of wear determines when new shoes are needed.

**Ringbone:** A deposit of calcium that occurs at the coffin joint (low ringbone), at the pastern joint (high ringbone), or on either pastern bone other than at a joint (nonarticular ringbone).

**Rocker-toe shoe:** A shoe that tilts up in the front to hasten breakover and ease stress on the foot.

**Rolled-toe shoe:** A shoe that is thinner at the front edge to hasten breakover and ease stress on the foot.

**Run-under foot:** A foot on which the heels grow forward rather than downward.

**Sealant:** A protective coating applied to the hoof wall to reduce moisture loss through evaporation.

**Sesamoid bones (proximal):** The two small bones at the fetlock joint that act as a fulcrum for tendons and ligaments.

**Sesamoid bone (distal):** Same as navicular bone.

**Sheared heels:** A condition in which the horse's heels are uneven so that the two bulbs are not at the same height above the ground.

**Sickle-hocked:** Having the hind cannon bones pointing slightly forward rather than vertical.

**Sideline:** A rope arrangement used to hold up a horse's foot so it will stand still for shoeing.

**Sole bruise:** Minor damage caused by compression of any area of the sensitive sole, causing bleeding into the tissues.

**Splint:** A lump of calcium deposited to repair damage when the ligaments attaching the splint bones to the cannon bones are torn.

**Splint bone:** One of the slender triangular bones on each side of the cannon bone, which add to the articulating surface for the knee or hock.

**Square-toe shoe:** A shoe that is flattened at the front edge to hasten breakover and ease stress on the foot.

**Synovial fluid:** A transparent, viscous lubricating fluid secreted by the membranes of the joint capsule, the bursas, and the synovial sheath.

**Synovial sheath:** The protective covering of a tendon.

**Tendon:** A strong, inelastic cord that transfers the contractive pull of a muscle to a bone, producing movement.

**Thrush:** An anaerobic fungus infection that attacks the frog of a horse's foot.

**Toeing in:** Having the feet pointing inward rather than straight ahead.

**Toeing out:** Having the feet pointing outward instead of straight ahead.

**Trailer:** The heel of a horseshoe that has been bent to point sideways away from the foot instead of following the line of the heel. Usually applied on the outside branch of a shoe.

**Twitch:** A set of pincers or a handle with a loop of rope or chain attached that is tightened around a horse's upper lip as a restraining device.

**Weighted shoes:** Shoes with extra weight added either all over or on one portion of the shoe.

**White line:** The line between the sole and the hoof wall.

**Wry foot:** A hoof whose shape is distorted with a corresponding bend of the horn tubules.

# Bibliography

BOOKS

Amos, LeRoy. *Limbs of the Equine.* Navarre, OH: Ashberry Acres Pulications, 1986.

Beaston, Bud. *The Master Farrier.* Sperry, Oklahoma: Oklahoma Farrier's College, 1975.

Butler, Doug. *The Principles of Horseshoeing II.* Maryville, MO: Doug Butler, 1985.

Frandson, R. D. *Anatomy and Physiology of Farm Animals.* Philadelphia: Lea and Febiger, 1981.

Hill, Cherry. *From the Center of the Ring.* Pownal, VT: Garden Way, 1988.

Jacob, Stanley W. *Structure and Function in Man.* Philadelphia: W. B. Saunders, 1974.

Rooney, James R. *The Lame Horse: Causes, Symptoms, and Treatment.* North Hollywood, CA: Wilshire, 1974.

Simpson, J. Scott. *The Identification, Analysis, and Correction of Gait Faults in Horses.* Walla Walla, WA: Last Chance Ranch Enterprises, 1989.

MAGAZINES

*American Farriers Journal.* Laux Company, 63 Great Road, Maynard, MA 01754. Bi-monthly.

*Anvil.* P.O. Box 1810, Georgetown, CA 95634-1810. Monthly.

*Equus.* P.O. Box 932, Farmingdale, NY 11737

# Index